Ready to Launch

Practical steps for starting
your business

M. A. Novak, MBA

Contents

Introduction

Like many entrepreneurs I caught the business bug at a young age. I made my first foray into self-employment when I was five by selling my crayon artwork door-to-door for two cents. The neighbors in my suburban cul-de-sac were happy to hand over their spare change if only to get me out of their doorways.

Unfortunately, my mom wasn't as proud of my entrepreneurial activities as I was. She introduced me to an important business concept, the refund. I swallowed my five-year-old pride and returned the change to my customers. Little did they know that I would go on to have some success as an illustrator and an artist. Had they kept their purchased works of art, those crayon scribbles could have been the best two cents my customers ever spent.

From my early business venture, I learned three valuable lessons. First, I learned that entrepreneurship takes courage. To come up with an idea, make it reality, and present it to the marketplace isn't easy. Naysayers are plentiful. Self-doubt is always present. Doors do get slammed in your face.

It takes guts to put your career and reputation on the line. But entrepreneurs don't give up. They overcome challenges, not run from them. Entrepreneurs must trust their intuition and skills even if no one else does. Ultimately, to reap the rewards of business ownership, entrepreneurs must have courage to choose a life that is unique, exciting and filled with exploration.

Second, I learned that profits can disappear quickly. A penny earned today is a penny gone tomorrow. Learning from business owners' experiences and following established business practices is a key factor in running a successful business.

Missteps come with owning a business, but with basic business knowledge, proper planning, careful financial management, and well-defined organization entrepreneurs can maximize profits rather than mitigating losses. And new businesses can thrive.

The third lesson I took away from my art sales experience is that we need to view the world with eyes that see a world of opportunity—not obstacles. Every day is an adventure to be faced with a brave and confident heart.

Entrepreneurs are driven by many things:
- passion
- necessity
- the desire to be your own boss
- the urge to compete in the marketplace
- the desire to invent something of value to others
- the need for flexibility
- an interest in using industry knowledge differently

Each business idea is as unique as the entrepreneur behind it. When skills, knowledge and ambition intersect and the timing is right, go boldly into the world of self-employment. Become the master of your passions—Invent, build, organize, and LAUNCH!

Chapter 1:
Building your business from an idea

We all have ideas. We keep notebooks of product sketches, story plot lines, music snippets—anything that gives our brain a jolt. Ideas may be born out of practicality such as improving on a product or process to make it work more efficiently. Others may be pure novelty—think plastic vomit and whoopee cushions. Businesses are built on ideas—but not everyone with an idea starts a business. To determine if your business idea could be the next big thing, start by doing research and applying a little introspection.

Define your business idea

Determine what you want to produce, provide as a service, or sell and if there is a viable customer base for your product or service. If you have a laundry list of ideas, narrow the list down to those that excite you and are most likely to appeal to customers. Strong positive feelings about your business idea will help you stay motivated while you build your business.

As you look through your idea list, ask yourself some basic questions to get started:

- What makes my business idea unique?
- Who is the target customer?
- What problem am I solving for them?
- Does the product have features that make it easier to use?
- Can I offer a service that is hard to find?
- Will the product or service fill a niche?
- Can I offer the product or service at a competitive price?
- What resources do I need to create the product of offer the service (funding, staff, suppliers, tech)?
- Do I have the skills and knowledge to create the product or perform the service?
- Am I passionate enough to commit the time, money, and energy?
- Do I have (or can I build) the right network/partners to succeed?

The answers to these questions will help you determine whether you have a product or service that is unique in the marketplace and whether you have the capabilities to bring it to market. This is just an initial review of your business idea and delving deeper into the details will come later.

When you have a completed list, show it to family and friends. Expect some laughter, some negativity, but also some valuable insight into the potential for your business idea to be successful. Listen and refine. Refine and listen. Give your idea form and shape. Then set it aside. If you are still gung-ho about moving forward after receiving feedback from your sounding board, then it's time to take the next step.

So, what is the next step? Research, research, and more research. It is essential to understand the industry your product will compete in. If your product or service is in demand, the market has few competitors, and start-up costs are low, the market is said to have low barriers to entry. Low barriers to entry in a market means introducing your product or service to the market is easier.

If the market for your product or service has high barriers to entry, meaning it is already crowded with well-entrenched business providers or start-up costs are high, you will need more resources to enter the market. To learn about the market, make friends with the Internet, the library and trade journals. A quick search can provide invaluable competitor and market research.

Know your competitors

Using Internet search engines, run a search on the product or service you hope to sell. The result will include a list of businesses selling the same or similar products. You can refine your search based on specific criteria that you have identified as important. You may want to search for companies in your community, state or other geographic location.

Visit each competitor's website to learn details about how each company operates. And jot down how each company markets its products. That will be useful later when you are developing a marketing plan. If a competitor is publicly traded, check their website for annual reports. These reports provide valuable information about company history, plans for growth, and profitability. You also can use online fee-based resources such as Hoovers and Dun & Bradstreet to learn more about the competitors you have identified.

And don't forget to peruse traditional media, such as the business section of national and local newspapers and trade journals. Here, you will learn the latest business moves your competitors are making.

Understand trends

The next step in your research is to look for trends that would impact your business. On the web, news sources, blogs, discussion boards, social media, business networking sites, and AI tools provide insight into what's hot in a market—and what's not. Review positive and negative feedback. Engage in conversation with others involved in the industry you are researching. Ask questions, when possible, to gauge where experts feel the industry is moving.

Read, read, and read! Online and traditional publications offer a wealth of trend information. Read daily news updates, newsletters and trade magazines to spot trends. Visit your local bookstore and see how your product or business is represented in magazines. If the racks are stocked with magazines featuring your product or industry, the outlook for entering the market may be good. If your type of business owns even a small corner of the rack, that may be a positive sign of a successful niche market.

When doing your research, pay attention to lifestyle changes that may impact your product. For example, if you have invented a new lawn chemical, but the trend is toward greener lawn care, the timing may not be right for your business. Ultimately, knowing where a market is heading makes it easier to determine if and when to enter the market.

Learn the business

A key to success in an industry is to understand how the day-to-day operations of the business you hope to start operates. If you are an industry insider, having worked as an employee of a company that produces your product or service, you have a head start.

You may already have a good understanding of the business landscape in which you will be operating. You may even have developed relationships that you can capitalize on when you leave the company to go out on your own. If you are not currently employed in a business similar to the one you hope to manage, your interest in starting a business in the industry means you are likely to have an idea of how the business functions. In either case, it is valuable to stay current about issues that affect the industry and learn what tactics businesses take to address the issues.

To learn more about how businesses similar to the business you hope to start function, attend industry conferences and trade shows, join trade groups, and talk with others. Make connections. By positioning yourself at events frequented by industry insiders you will not only learn what business tools and processes are common in the industry, you will gain valuable contacts.

During my early years as a web consultant, I attended educational seminars around the country. I dedicated my mornings to learning about new technologies and planning tools but spent my afternoons trading business cards with other professionals in the field. We discussed industry issues, shared ideas and opened the door to future communication. I still have those cards and can call on those experts when needed.

Finding a mentor is another great way to learn the ins and outs of the business you are interested in. A mentor should be someone you are comfortable going to with questions. He or she should be your cheerleader and coach. A mentor helps you learn from your mistakes and encourages your efforts. A successful mentorship could lead to a valuable partnership after your business gets off the ground. Here's a short list of characteristics you can look for in a mentor:

- Is mature and experienced in the industry
- Collaborates with you on projects to help you hone your business skills
- Models ethical behavior
- Encourages you and provides sincere feedback
- Motivates you to try new tasks and guides you in those endeavors

Chapter 2:
Tools for researching business ideas

Your business idea has grown from a sentence written on the back of a napkin to the start of a business plan refined with input from your sounding board, mentor, and your own research.

You're not quite ready to launch yet. Now, it's important to understand the deeper market, financial, and environmental factors that can impact your business. The goal of this phase on your start-up journey is to gain a big-picture understanding of how your business idea fits into the market and what internal and external influences could impact your success.

With this knowledge, you'll be able to better position your business, plan for resource needs, and mitigate the risks you might face as you enter the market.

The common business analysis tools found in this chapter are useful to capture your thoughts and build a roadmap to help you make smarter decisions, communicate clearly with investors or partners, and avoid costly mistakes as you build your idea into a business. When using these tools:

- Be specific in your responses. For example, include competitor names and exact marketing channels when evaluating these elements.

17

- Document your research so you know where every number, detail, or assumption came from.
- Revisit and revise your results as you gather more data.
- Connect the dots to determine how your results influence or impact each other and how they can help define your business plan.

PESTEL

PESTEL is an acronym for Political, Economic, Social, Technological, Environmental, Legal. This framework helps you explore the external environment and industry dynamics that could impact your business.

One way to use this framework is to create a grid with one column for each of the six research areas. Then do the following:
- In each column list the top three to five forces that could impact your business idea. These could be regulations, laws, technology changes, or current events.
- For each force, rate the **Impact** as Low, Medium or High and the **Uncertainty** and Low or High.
- In your grid, highlight High-Impact/High-Uncertainty items. These are areas worth investigating further. High-uncertainty items are areas to evaluate to

determine if they pose a risk to success of your business while High-Impact items could bolster your business. These are your areas to watch and possible opportunities.

Porter's Five Forces

This framework helps identify the competitive forces at play in an industry including:
- competition
    - number of competitors
    - similar products or services
    - industry growth potential
    - industry costs
- threats of new businesses joining the market
    - startup costs
    - customer loyalty to existing businesses
    - distribution options
    - regulations
- supplier power over pricing (few suppliers with limited substitutes versus multiple suppliers)
- customer power over pricing and quality
    - fewer purchasers vs. many purchasers
    - complexity of switching from on product to another
    - customer price sensitivity

- availability of substitute products or services (is it easy to find a similar product for a lower price?)

To use this framework, start by creating a grid. Examine these competitive forces and rate their impact on the industry. Based on your analysis you can determine the potential for your business or service to be profitable in an industry, and where you could face challenges and would need to mitigate risks.

Break-even analysis

When starting a business, one of the most important questions to ask is: *How much do I need to sell to cover my costs?* That is where a break-even analysis comes in. This tool helps you find the point at which your sales equal your expenses—when you are not losing money, but you are not yet making a profit either.

Knowing your break-even point gives you a realistic picture of what it takes to keep your business running. Many first-time business owners underestimate how much they need to sell, or they set prices too low to cover their costs. A break-even analysis forces you to think carefully about expenses and sales targets before you launch your business and helps you make better decisions about pricing, costs, and growth.

Here's the basic formula:

Break-Even Point (in units) = Fixed Costs ÷ (Selling Price per Unit – Variable Cost per Unit)

- **Fixed costs** are expenses that do not change no matter how much you sell, such as rent, insurance, or salaries.
- **Variable costs** are expenses that change depending on sales, like raw materials, shipping, or packaging.
- **Selling price per unit** is what you charge your customer for a product or service.

For example, if you discover that you need to sell 1,000 units per month to breakeven but your market research shows you can realistically only sell 600 units, you know you must adjust your plan. You might raise your price, lower your costs, or rethink your business model. Without this calculation, you could move forward with a plan that isn't sustainable.

Scenario planning

Scenario planning helps business owners prepare for uncertainty by identifying "what-if" situations and planning options for working through those situations. The goal of scenario planning is to future-proof your business so you can respond swiftly as the industry changes.

During scenario planning, you can use the information gained from your previous research around industry dynamics, competitive forces, and risks to visualize possible future scenarios. Scenarios can include both positive and negatives factors that can impact an industry.

Once those scenarios have been developed, you can create plans for addressing each one including resource adjustments, shifts in strategy, product development planning, sales and marketing options and financial shifts.

SWOT analysis

SWOT stands for strengths, weaknesses, opportunities, and threats. This evaluation tool will help you gain a better understanding of your business and where it stands against competitors. The SWOT analysis can be used at many points during the business life cycle, but in the early stages it can help you evaluate your chance for successfully launching your business.

First, write a list of your business' strengths. Since your business is still in the planning stages, record your perceived strengths. Include any strengths that may set you apart from competitors or make it easier for you to enter the market. For example:

- Do you hold a patent to a unique product or technology?
- Do you have a solid reputation in your industry?
- Can you offer the product or service at a lower price than other businesses?

Next, make a list of your business's weaknesses. When you know your weaknesses, you can address them head-on rather than allowing them to become roadblocks to your success.

- Do you have limited financial resources to support your business?
- Are you lacking in industry experience?
- Do you have limited time to operate your business?

Now, move on to opportunities. Analyze the external environment that your business would operate in. Write down trends, regulations, and demographic and customer factors that can work in your favor. Your goal is to generate a list of opportunities that can lead to business growth and profit.

Finally, examine threats in the external environment that could impact your company.

- Are there similar or substitute products already offered?

- Are the barriers to entering the market high? High entry barriers may include government regulations, high start-up costs, and strong customer loyalty to established companies.

Once you know the threats, you can minimize the impact on your company through careful strategic planning.

The results of the SWOT analysis will not only help you determine if you want to enter the industry but will provide you with guidance on how to position your company if you decide to move forward with your business idea.

Know yourself

Running a business is a challenge. It can bring joy and prosperity but also lead to stress and financial strain. Before you jump in, take a step back. You've assessed your competitors and the industry and learned the business. Now assess yourself. Ask yourself three questions and answer them honestly.

1. Do you have the education and certifications necessary to operate the business? Many service businesses require special licenses or certifications to operate. For example, if your dream is to open a home daycare, most states require special licensing. You may also need First Aid, CPR, or early childhood development certifications. To offer accounting

services you may need a college degree and CPA certification.

2. Do you have the skills to perform the business responsibilities? For example, if you want to provide marketing services, your customers expect you to have experience in different aspects of marketing. Also, as a business owner, understanding bookkeeping, selling, and customer service will help you operate the business effectively.

3. Do you have the personal qualities that will make you a successful business owner? Business owners benefit by being motivated, flexible, and confident in their abilities. Other qualities that will improve your chances of success include the ability to handle stress and long hours and the ability to make difficult decisions.

Ultimately, a desire to succeed, commitment to building your business, and good timing will drive your success.

Example: Finding a niche

A client that was nearing retirement from a public service career wanted to try his hand at owning a private business. He had a longtime interest in raising plants native to Minnesota.

It was a niche industry that he had been studying while still employed.

As he wound down his full-time career, he invested time in learning about the nursery business and in training to produce plants. He made contacts with natural resource experts, volunteered in seed picking and planting events, and visited local nurseries to learn how to operate a greenhouse. He read newspapers and trade magazines to learn about the industry.

What he found through his research excited him. Research indicated that the market for plant products in Minnesota was strong. Family-operated businesses generated billions in yearly sales. Retail sales, which encompass roadside markets, specialized growers, landscape supply centers, and garden centers, accounted for almost $500 million in sales. Horticulture and agricultural production, which included growing trees, shrubs, perennials, annuals and potted plants, totaled an estimated $350 million.

Gross sales for nursery and landscape companies were expected to increase 30 to 50 percent in the next five years. The agricultural production segment, which includes native plants, was increasing at the fastest rate. Industry trends also favored growth:

- Consumers were focused on environmental issues.
- Community groups and non-profits promoted native plants as an environmentally friendly, low maintenance option to traditional landscaping plants.

- Urban communities used native plants to address water runoff issues.
- Gardeners used native plants to repel pests and to attract helpful insects.
- Some communities modified weed laws to allow natural landscaping.

With the potential for success looking positive, my client invested time in understanding the complex competitive landscape.

His competition included:

- Suppliers of bulk seed for conservation projects. In Minnesota, there were at least 19 seed houses supplying bulk seed for restoration and conservation projects.
- Traditional nurseries and flower shops. There were at least 30 nurseries in the state that sold a combination of native and non-native plants.

After several years spent learning the industry and countless hours toiling in his plant beds, my client was confident that he could operate successfully within the niche native plant market.

To be absolutely positive he prepared a SWOT analysis to guide his business and marketing plans. Based on the results of the SWOT analysis, my client realized he would need to start small to best take advantage of his strengths while lessening the impact of his weaknesses.

Since he was highly knowledgeable about growing native plants, he would single-handedly take on the plant cultivation responsibility. Without labor expenses, he could split his limited financial resources between creating basic marketing materials and purchasing supplies to help grow his business.

He would focus his sales efforts on the contacts he generated at local gardening expos and events and would apply any income he generated towards expansion.

He also would also make connections with organizations committed to environmental issues so that he could capitalize on the trend towards "green" landscaping.

With his roadmap for success in mind, my client launched his business when the market was ripe for his product.

Chapter 3:
Getting your ducks in a row

Businesses are built from the bottom. An idea that may seem unshaped, even disorderly, is given form by careful assessment, planning and building. Different structures suit different types of businesses. Choosing a structure for your business is based on your business's unique attributes and the tax benefits and liability protection that each structure provides.

If you have questions about which business structure best fits your situation, a business attorney or accountant can give you a thorough review of the pros and cons, but here's a general overview.

Sole proprietorship

If you are your business's sole owner and it is not incorporated or registered as a limited liability company or corporation, it is considered a sole proprietorship. Freelancers and people who work on a contract or commission basis often fall into the sole proprietorship category. This is a simple and inexpensive way to structure a business that requires little paperwork to establish.

Sole proprietorships are required to register a business name if the name for your company doesn't include your first and last names. For example, if your company is called Joe Smith Plumbing, you do not need to register the name. However, if your company is called Smith Plumbing, this name is considered a fictitious or assumed name and must be registered. As a part of registration, you may be required to publish a notice of registration in your local newspaper. The goal of this requirement is to protect consumers so they can identify the owner of a company if the owner's name is not in the title.

Registration is important because banks won't open accounts for assumed/fictitious names that are not registered. You also may have difficulty enforcing contracts and other legal documents.

If you choose to structure your company as a sole proprietorship, be aware that the business is viewed as an extension of you, the individual. All your business assets and liabilities are viewed as personal assets and liabilities. You are not required to pay corporate income taxes, but instead you must file a Schedule C form when you complete your personal taxes. Because the government doesn't recognize a distinction between you and your business under this structure, legal action against your company puts your personal assets at risk. As your sole proprietorship becomes successful or if you are seeking financing, you may want to register as a Limited Liability Company.

Limited liability company

Structuring your company as a limited liability company (LLC) offers liability protection available to corporations, meaning the company's members cannot be held personally responsible for the company's debts or claims against the company. Because the company is separate from the owner, it is important to keep company records, debts and assets separate from your own. LLCs are simpler to operate than their incorporated peers. Formalities such as regular board meetings and the associated meeting minutes are not required.

LLCs also are not subject to double taxation (paying both corporate and personal taxes) because taxes are paid by the individual or individuals in the company on their personal tax forms. LLCs provide flexibility in how profits are passed through to individuals in a company.

To register as an LLC, you will need to prepare and file articles of organization with your state's Secretary of State. This is a formal document that includes your company's unique name, address, some specifics about the company and information about the company's management structure.

Requirements for the articles of organization and additional required materials vary by state so check your state's Secretary of State office for documents and information.

Partnership

If you choose to go into business with another person, you may consider setting up a partnership. The partnership structure works well if another person has expertise that complements your own and could benefit the business. The partner also might have financial resources to help build the business. No legal documentation is required to form a partnership, though it is wise to write out a partnership agreement.

Partnership arrangements are either general partnerships or limited partnerships. General partnerships don't provide either partner with liability protection. Therefore, each partner's personal assets can be at risk if a judgment is made against the company.

In a limited partnership, only one partner's personal assets are at risk. The partner who takes on the responsibility for risk generally manages the company, while the other partner just provides some investment capital or advice.

Partnerships can work well for companies just starting out, but as your company grows you could consider becoming an LLC or corporation to protect your assets.

Corporation

If you want to create your business as a separate legal entity from yourself to avoid personal liability for claims made against the company, setting it up as a corporation is a way to achieve that goal.

Corporations have shareholders, people who own stock in the company. Shareholders may be the owners of the corporation, outside investors and company employees. When the company earns a profit, the shareholders share in that profit through dividends issued by the company.

Corporations can enter into legal contracts and financial agreements and are held responsible for any debts incurred during the course of business.

Corporations can be set up in several ways, including as S corporations, C corporations, and non-profits. Each type of corporation has different tax requirements so it is wise to discuss each structure's tax implications with an accountant or tax attorney.

If you choose to set up your business as a corporation you will need to file the appropriate paperwork with state and regulatory agencies and pay the associated fees.

To file as a corporation, you will also prepare Articles of Incorporation, sometimes called Articles of Organization. This document filed in the state of incorporation includes basic information about your corporation such as the company name, the owner's name, whether the corporation is for profit or not-for-profit, and the corporation's stock structure.

The corporation's founders develop bylaws, which are rules for the corporation. The corporation must also meet certain requirements on an ongoing basis to prove corporate status.

These include holding annual board meetings and keeping meeting minutes on file, issuing stock certificates to shareholders and electing directors to make decisions and carry out company responsibilities.

Writing a business plan

Once you choose a business structure that meets your needs, the next step is to write a business plan. The business plan serves two purposes:

- First, it is a resource for leaders within your company to follow throughout the business's lifespan. It provides the blueprint for your organization by outlining company goals and how you will achieve them. It is also a reference document that will help you and your employees make business planning decisions based on the core business ideas included in your business plan.
- Second, the business plan is a resource for others to use to learn about your company. For example, if you

need outside funding to launch your business, creditors and investors can review your business plan to learn about your financial position and funding needs. If you bring a partner into your business, that person can review your business plan to ensure that you are both on the same page about how the business operates.

Each business plan is unique to the company that creates it. Length and content may vary based on the intended audience. If you are writing for investors, focus on the financials. If you are writing for creditors, include information that explains how each creditor will be repaid.

Because your company is a growing and changing business, your business plan will also change, but by including key information about your company you will always have a jumping off point for making key decisions.

Keep your business plan concise by only including relevant information—no filler. Bullet points, headings and short paragraphs make for easier reading. Some common elements of a business plan include the following:

The executive summary

The executive summary is a short overview of your business plan that entices the reader to read the entire plan. It describes your business concept including a product or service description, the market you will serve, and your business's unique attributes (how you will compete against other similar businesses in the industry.)

- Include successes you have experienced, even if they seem small. Be as specific as possible.
- The summary shouldn't repeat what other sections of your business plan cover but it should cover all important points from the rest of the plan.
- Also include general information such as the company's legal structure, history, and office locations.
- To put a face on your business, a listing of owners and key employees is also worth including.

If you will be seeking investors, your executive summary also should contain your company's key financial highlights such as sales, profits, cash flows, return on investment, and growth. You should also explain the capital you will need to build your business and how the loan or investment will be used. Also explain what investors will receive in return (e.g., equity in the company) and what your plans are to grow the company in the future.

Your executive summary should include your company's mission statement. The mission statement is a carefully crafted sentence or short paragraph that explains what your business hopes to achieve. Describe your product or services, your target market, and your company ideals in broad terms that will stand up to the test of time.

Business profile

In this section of the business plan provide detailed information about your company's history, ownership structure, company locations, and your start-up costs. Start-up costs could include costs to develop your product, license fees, insurance costs, rental fees, and marketing costs. Also include any capital you have available when you launch the business.

Products or services

Tell readers what you sell and why it would be a benefit for them to purchase your product or service. If you have developed a product or service to meet a market need, mention that here. Explain what features make your product or service different from the competition and why those differences are important to consumers.

In this section, also explain if your product is in the development phase or if it is ready for market. If you are seeking investors for a start-up business you may not yet have a fully functioning product. Make sure to mention if a product prototype is available and include your plans for developing the final product. If you hold a patent or copyright for the product, mention that as well.

Market analysis

One business success factor is knowing your market well. In your business plan, define characteristics of the market where you will be offering your product or service. Use the results of your business analysis (SWOT, PESTEL, break-even point) to help complete the market analysis section. List industry trends you have identified and how they are affecting market growth. Include past growth rates, current sales, industry size, and industry growth forecasts. Also include any regulatory restrictions on your industry and costs involved to abide by those restrictions.

Next include information about your target market. The target market is the specific market segment or niche where you will offer your product. Include demographic information about your target market such as age, gender, and geographic location—be as specific as possible. Also, include the market size and growth rate. The more defined your market is, the easier it is to measure your potential for success in that market.

Don't forget your competitors. Include an overview of main industry competitors and list their strengths and weaknesses. Include major and secondary competitors. If you have access to competitors' sales figures, include that information as well. Explain how you will compete against your competitors to gain market share. Include pricing plans, marketing strategies and promotional campaigns you hope to undertake, efficiencies you have identified, and customer service initiatives you will put in place to meet customers' needs.

Financials

It is important to have a good grasp on your company's financial health even if you are in the early stages of launching your business. Investors, potential partners, creditors, even future employees want to know what capital you have available and what additional financial resources you will need to operate.

They'll also feel more comfortable supporting your business when you prove to have a clear understanding of the business's financial position. If your business is just getting off the ground, supply forecasted financial information. Make sure it is realistic and well-researched based on the results of businesses similar to yours, industry trends, and your own knowledge and experience.

The following financial information should be included in the financials section for a 12-month period:

Balance sheets

Balance sheets show a company's financial position at a certain point in time, for example at the end of the year. The balance sheet contains a list of assets and liabilities, and owner's equity (the company's net worth). The assets and liabilities plus equity must balance (assets = liabilities + Shareholders equity).

Assets listed on the balance sheet include:

- Cash
- Accounts receivable (money owed to the company)
- Value of product inventories
- Equipment, land and buildings

Liabilities listed on the balance sheet include:

- Accounts payable (money you owe to others)
- Notes payable
- Accruals (charges incurred but not yet paid)
- Long-term debt such as leases
- Accrued income taxes

Equity includes common stock issued to raise money for the company and retained earnings, which are funds the company keeps rather than paying it out as dividends to shareholders.

Income statements

An income statement shows the revenue your company has earned and the expenses it has incurred over a specific time period, usually monthly or quarterly. It is helpful in determining your business's profitability.

The income statement can take two formats, multi-step or single-step. The single-step income statement is the simplest form, requiring fewer calculations to determine net income. The version you choose is based on the level of detail you or your investors need to evaluate your business.

In general, the income statement starts with a record of revenue. It may include the following:

- Sales revenue made by selling goods or services
- Interest revenue
- Non-operating revenue from the sale of assets

Next is a record of all expenses. Expenses may include the following:

- Costs of goods sold (this is the costs associated with selling a product)
- Operating costs such as salaries, advertising, utilities, depreciation, and other day-to-day operating expenses
- Interest expenses that you pay on loans, mortgages or any other borrowed funds

After determining the total expenses, these are subtracted from the total revenue to determine your net income before taxes. Next, list any taxes owed to local, state or federal governments and subtract this amount from the net income before taxes. The result or bottom line is called the net income, the income that is available to common shareholders or to owners if your company is a sole proprietorship or partnership.

Amortization and depreciation

As mentioned above, amortization and depreciation are included on the income statement. Amortization refers to allocating the cost of an intangible asset over the asset's lifetime. Assets are anything of value owned by a company. Intangible assets are items of value that cannot be touched or seen such as a mortgage, patent, or copyright. For example, if you have a 30-year mortgage on a building you may pay $2,000 a month for 30 years.

Depreciation is used to allocate the cost of a tangible asset such as machinery over the asset's useful life. A company uses specific calculations to determine how to depreciate its assets. An accountant can provide options for how best to depreciate your company's assets.

Cash flow statements

The cash flow statement includes a breakdown of a company's cash position during a set time period, usually monthly or quarterly. It is used to determine if a company is financially stable and can repay its debts. It is broken down into three sections: Operating activities, investing activities, and financing activities.

- Operating Activities are those that generate and use funds during a company's day-to-day operations.

- Investing activities are those that support the company's long-term operations such as purchasing buildings, equipment and property.
- Financing activities include loans, stock transactions and any other activities between a company and its investors and shareholders.

If you don't feel comfortable creating the financial documents, popular accounting software is available to do so. Document templates may also be available on the Internet. You can also contact an accountant to create financial documents. It is important to be as accurate as possible.

Protecting your intellectual property

Protecting your logos, company names, products, and marketable processes that make your company unique is an important consideration when starting a business. The legal name for the creative works generated by a company is intellectual property. The legal system provides businesses with means to protect intellectual property through patents, copyrights, and trademarks issued by the United States Patent and Trademark Office.

Patents

If you have invented a product or process and want to prevent others from making or selling the same product or using your process, you can apply for a patent. Patents grant you property rights to the invention or process usually for 20 years from the date your application is filed. The length of a patent varies depending on the type of patent you receive. The three types of patents are:

- utility patents for inventions and process,
- design patents for ornamental designs of manufactured products and,
- plant patents for the discovery or invention of plants.

A maintenance fee paid to the government is required to keep a patent active. To receive a patent, your invention or process must meet the following criteria:

- It must be useful, meaning it has a useful purpose and operates as intended.
- It must be novel which means the item you hope to patent isn't in use already. A description of the item also must not have appeared anywhere more than one year before you applied for your patent.
- It must not be obvious; meaning the item you want to patent must be different from existing processes and inventions. Using a common item and changing it in a minor way won't earn you a patent.

Trademarks and service marks

If your company has a logo, unique name, catch word, or phrase that identifies your products and distinguishes them in the marketplace, you can seek trademark protection from the U.S. Patent and Trademark Office. If the identifiers refer to a service instead of a product you would apply for a service mark. If you are granted a trademark or service mark, other businesses can't use marks that are similar to yours. Your marks are protected even if you don't register them as long as you actively use them in the marketplace. However, registration provides an added level of legitimacy to your claim for ownership of the marks.

Copyrights

A copyright protects authored works such as books, music, and literary works. Copyright protection means the work is registered with the Copyright Office of the Library of Congress and the owner has exclusive rights to determine how the work is used and reproduced.

Copyright only protects the expression of the ideas contained in the work, not the subject matter. For example, if an author writes a travel book about Florida, other writers can't copy her words or reproduce the writing for distribution. They can certainly write their own books about traveling in Florida.

Authored works don't need to be registered to be copyrighted. Any work that is tangible, meaning it exists in a recorded form and is original, is copyrighted. Registering the works provides greater legal protection because it proves that the work was created on a specific date. This will be important if someone copies the work or challenges its originality.

Copyrights pose a unique challenge with the proliferation of online and AI-generated content. With the click of the mouse anyone can copy text and images and use them in their own materials. But images and text on the Internet are copyrighted unless they specifically say otherwise.

This is a sticky issue for business owners that may want to grab an attractive image or catchy text or have AI generate content for use in marketing materials.

If you can't verify that the image or text is copyright-free and available for general use, don't use it.

Loose ends

If you sell a product or service that is taxable, you are required to pay taxes quarterly. For filing tax-related documents you will need a Tax ID number for your business. The most common number used by small businesses is individual social security numbers or Employer ID numbers (EIN).

Using your social security number as your Tax ID requires no additional paperwork. However, if you are uncomfortable using your social security number for business purposes you can file for an EIN directly through the IRS website.

A Tax ID number may be required for businesses that meet any of the following criteria:

- You have employees
- You are a corporation or partnership
- You file employment, excise, or alcohol, tobacco and firearms tax forms
- You withhold taxes on income, other than wages, paid to a non-resident alien
- Certain banking and financial transactions

It's a good idea to consult with a tax professional to determine the best approach for your business.

Example: What's the plan?

Bonnie, a fresh-out-of-school MBA graduate, was dissatisfied with corporate life's slow pace. She was a marketer for an insurance company where her opportunities for professional growth were stagnant. She wanted more for her career.

Luckily, fate intervened. While on a weekend outing, Bonnie met a business owner looking for a marketer to help raise the profile of his start-up business. It was a part-time contract position that would fit into the hours around her full-time job. Bonnie jumped at the chance.

Bonnie saw the contract opportunity as a sign that there were possibilities beyond the walls of her office cube and she laid the groundwork to leave the corporate world behind her.

A couple of nights a week, Bonnie worked on projects for the business owner. The projects were small—a postcard, a brochure, and a website—but were enough to help him establish his business in the marketplace. While she was helping the new business during its first year, Bonnie also saved extra money from her full-time job that she would use to fund her exit from her workplace.

After she felt comfortable with her savings and potential for success, Bonnie pulled the plug on her job and became an entrepreneur.

While the move gave her more time to help her new client, she soon found herself without work seven months out of the year due to the seasonal nature of her client's business.

To fill the gap, she launched her own company to provide a full-plate of marketing services to non-profit and small business clients. Services included project planning, creative design, print materials development, web design, web maintenance, and more. Businesses could use these services one time or on an ongoing basis.

Business trickled in, generated by word-of-mouth marketing and answering help wanted ads on contract job websites. But business wasn't booming and the owner was spread thin trying to market the business and keep up-to-date on all the latest marketing and technology trends.

Bonnie studied search engine optimization, looked for classes in project management, and explored new trends in marketing materials while trying to serve her clients from a variety of disparate industries. She needed a break.

So, she took a step back. Prior to starting the business, the motivated business owner made a mistake. She didn't write a business plan. As a result, Bonnie lacked an understanding of the forces at play in the market and didn't configure her product offerings accordingly. She threw everything she had at customers, whether they wanted it or not. She thought she was offering services her clients would snap up, but she was wrong.

The state of the market

When Bonnie launched her business, the economy was sliding into a recession. Small business owners and non-profits—Bonnie's target market—were cutting marketing budgets to fill their budget gaps due to funding losses.

These companies turned to electronic media to communicate with their constituents and clients. Blogs and websites took the place of print marketing tactics. The traditional marketing services Bonnie offered, such as brochure development, newsletter design and communication planning were low-demand services.

The company did have a web design specialty since Bonnie had found earlier success as an independent web designer and hoped to capitalize on that skill set again.

However, the market for web designers had changed dramatically since Bonnie last built a website. web design was not a money-maker. Template-based web design and web design services offered by hosting companies displaced independent web designers. User-friendly design tools opened web design to anyone willing to learn the software and the design techniques.

One market factor that remained consistent was that small-businesses and non-profits still outsourced their web design projects. The staff at these businesses were small and focused on servicing the core functions of the business. If they employed technical positions, those individuals were focused on maintaining company networks and computer hardware. While these companies understood the importance of using websites as a communication tool, many didn't want to devote staff time to maintaining the sites.

Bonnie noticed that her customers frequently requested advice relating to planning and managing websites. The project owners didn't always understand the technical jargon and development processes used in website projects. They looked to her as a middleman to make sense of the project. She did so usually at the same $15 an hour rate she charged for web design services.

The solution

After analyzing market conditions, the company's target market, and the competition, Bonnie developed a plan for refining her business offerings.

Since clients showed little interest in print marketing, she crossed that off her list. She continued to offer web design services but raised her starting rate to $30 per hour. She turned down work with pay rates below her minimum.

To attract high-value clients she teamed up with a programmer skilled in a variety of web technologies. While he took the lion's share of the profits, she was able to boost her bottom line, because she could take on more technically challenging and big-budget projects.

She also focused on project planning, analysis and management—skills she had honed while working as a marketer. She raised her pay rate for those services to $45 an hour. These services gave her a competitive advantage over companies and contractors that only performed the technical aspects of web design and development.

She supplemented the income generated through these services by offering ongoing website content maintenance. For a monthly fee of $300 or hourly rate of $45 she updated the text and graphics of client websites. Content maintenance included writing and editing services—her way of staying connected with her marketing past.

After making these changes, Bonnie's next step was to incorporate lessons learned into a business plan, then sell, sell, sell.

Chapter 4:
Financing your business

We can learn much from the little pink piggybank often gifted as a first tool towards financial awareness. Some piggybanks are plump and some are petite. Others are silent when coins drop and some oink up a storm. Some require a hammer to share the wealth while others just require a twist of the fingers.

A favorite is the elusive bottomless piggybank where money goes in and it comes right out again in a never-ending stream of cash.

Whether plastic or porcelain, these piggybanks provide their owners with a tiny bit of financial independence. Who hasn't found joy in the clink of a quarter dropping through the top slot followed by the euphoria of raiding the piggybank to buy a coveted trinket at the local dollar store?

As a business owner, knowing how to choose the right piggybank is an important step in building your business. Your financial success depends on it.

Start-up costs

The financing sources available to business owners range from banks to private investors to your own wallet. But before choosing a funding option for your business you will need to assess the costs you will incur to do business. It helps to start with a list.

Write down known business expenses. Include those that are a part of your start-up costs and those that are ongoing.

Your list may include common business costs such as insurance, legal fees, equipment expenses, and marketing costs.

Insurance

If you have employees, have visitors at your location, and have equipment to protect, you will need insurance. The basic categories of insurance include:
- property
- business interruption
- liability
- bonding of employees
- workers compensation
- group insurance for employees
- product liability

Tailor the insurance you purchase to the liability limitations associated with your enterprise and the scope of your business plan.

If you work out of your house, pay special attention to any changes that may need to be made to your homeowner's insurance. Your insurance agent can advise you about which policies are appropriate to your business needs.

If being frugal is a high priority, ask your agent about combining policies for a lower rate. For example, your buildings and equipment policy could be combined with your liability insurance. Also, consider joining a trade organization that provides access to insurance at discounted rates.

If you own a company that is difficult to insure, check with your state business association for programs available to companies unable to obtain insurance on the commercial market.

Start-up and ongoing legal fees

You may need a lawyer to establish the framework for your business including drafting the articles of incorporation, registering your business with the Secretary of State, filing your corporation's name, and addressing other legal concerns that arise.

You may have ongoing needs for a legal professional throughout the start-up phase and as you grow your business.

Issues around contracts, partnerships, intellectual property, and employees may require legal counsel. Plan for this expense as an ongoing need, even if the bulk of the expense is expected in the early stages of your business.

Taxes

Your business is subject to a variety of taxes including income tax, self-employment tax for people who work for themselves, and employment taxes such as Social Security, Medicare, and unemployment. A tax professional can advise you about which taxes your business must pay. Don't forget to include the cost for tax preparation.

Equipment

It is tempting when starting a business to load up on equipment. But debt for equipment will add to your overhead and may not be necessary to accomplish your business goals. When planning equipment purchases, estimate what you need to get your business off the ground and budget for any additional equipment as the need arises.

Marketing

Marketing is necessity for growing your business and unless you are a master at viral [low-cost and fast] marketing, it is rarely free. Marketing expenses can range from website development costs, email marketing management, paid Internet advertising, social media content creation, tradeshow marketing booths, and event coordination. Creating a marketing plan, covered in Chapter Six, will help you estimate marketing costs.

Misc.

When writing your cost list, be sure to include costs which are unique to your business and impact your bottom line. If you run a delivery service or lawn mowing business, you will incur gas and maintenance costs. If you own a greenhouse, gardening supplies, pots and fertilizer are important to include. Add any expense to your list that will impact your finances.

Forms of financing

Once you have a completed list of business costs, it's time to determine the best source of financing. Business owners have several options for financing based on the type of business, financial need, credit history and economic conditions.

Self-funded

If your start-up costs are minimal and you want to keep financial entanglements to a minimum, reaching into your own pockets to fund your business may be a good choice. Self-funded companies work well when your overhead is low, you have enough seed money to support most of your day-to-day operations for at least a year, and your debts are limited.

When you are footing the bill for your business, easing into your business while still working for an employer makes the financial transition easier. Began small by offering your service or product to a handful of customers. Work weekends, evenings, even holidays if you are able. Just make sure not to run your business on your current employer's time. You may end up jobless before you are ready to fully roll out your own business. While still working, it is easier to build upon your existing network of people. This network tends to break down after leaving a job.

If you choose the self-funding option, set up a business account where you can sock away funds to direct towards your business expenses. Keeping your personal and business finances separate means maintaining separate checking and savings accounts. Keeping separate accounts will ensure proper accounting come tax time.

Make sure if you are self-funding that you have enough money to cover your personal and business expenses. You don't want to fall behind on your personal bills while you are stocking up on office supplies for your business.

Third-party financing

Third party financing may be an option if you have a good credit rating and have start-up expenses and operating costs that you cannot cover out-of-pocket. Lending options and terms vary by bank but some financing plans to investigate include the following:

- ### *Small business administration loans*

  These loans are backed by the small business administration and can be used for start-up costs, real-estate purchases, day-to-day working capital needs, and inventory purchases. Visit SBA.gov on the web or your local bank for more information about SBA loans programs.

- ### *Lines of credit*

  Bank lines of credit can be used for short-term business needs, paying invoices, and meeting payroll if you have employees. Generally, credit lines can be used on a revolving basis.

- ***Bank loans***

    These lump sum loans can be used to make capital purchases, fund your business expansion, or cover costs associated with new business opportunities. Your business may need a successful track record before a bank will agree to loan you money.

- ***Grants***

    Grants for small businesses may include state and private grants. State grants often have specific purposes, such as encouraging job growth for an economically challenged area or they might be sector specific, for example bioscience-oriented. Check with the Department of Commerce or Economic Development Office in your state for a list of current funding programs. Private grants are offered by private companies, universities and foundations. A word of caution when looking for grants—do your research to avoid scam offers. Be wary of companies that offer grants or grant information for a fee and read all grant terms carefully.

Investor financing

Another option for funding your business is to seek investors. These are people or organizations who will provide you with

seed money with the expectation of receiving a financial
return on their investment. For small start-ups and businesses,
the options are somewhat limited. However, some investor
options to consider include:

- **Family and friends**
  People that are close to you and who support your
  vision may be willing to lend a financial hand.

- **Angel investors**
  These are individuals who may be willing to invest
  their own money in your business if they think it can
  return a profit. Investing in start-ups is risky so angel
  investors usually demand a high return on their
  investment. Expected returns of 20 percent or more
  are within reason. Board seats, a stake in your
  company, and the right to approve company decisions
  may also be on the angel investor's want list. Angel
  investors tend to invest in projects near their homes,
  so local "angels" are a good place to start. You can
  also search the Internet for links to Angel investors.

- **Crowdfunding**
  Crowdfunding raises money from large numbers of
  people through online platforms like Kickstarter,
  Indiegogo, or GoFundMe. Supporters contribute

small amounts in exchange for rewards, products, or sometimes equity in the business.

When working with investors remember to put all the terms of the relationship in writing. Even if you're just borrowing $500 from Uncle Joe, write it down. Memories are short and fuzzy. Written agreements help maintain good business relationships and in the case of friends and family good personal relationships.

If an investor opens his or her checkbook without providing a clear explanation of what he or she hopes to gain in return, proceed with caution. A friend, family member, or other investor may provide you with money several times as you get on your feet. You may see financial help as a gift, while the person handing you the money may intend it as an investment. Without an agreement in place that describes the terms of the arrangement, the deal may quickly turn sour.

If you aren't comfortable negotiating investor agreements, hire a lawyer. He or she can draft the agreement to cover the details and account for any eventuality. Wouldn't you rather see your siblings at a family reunion than in small claims court?

Responsible record-keeping

Maintaining financial health of your business is a combination of planning, organization and financial management. Many businesses have been sunk by bad record keeping. Here's an example:

A dear friend, who happens to be an accountant, hired a furnace expert to solve a heating problem. He came to her house, identified the problem and quickly got to work. The repair took a short time and her furnace worked marvelously. She thanked the repairman profusely and sent him on his way. He told her the bill would arrive in the mail.

Two weeks passed. No bill arrived. Another week passed and no bill. She called his office to remind him to send a bill. Another week passed and she called again. The bill never came. Bad business? Yes. Rare? No.

Ask a dozen people and you are likely to hear similar stories. If a client has to ask you multiple times for an invoice, your business is doomed. A few simple steps when you start your business will save you headaches and lost business down the road:

- **Use accounting software to record sales, create bills and pay invoices.**
  Accounting software does much of the record keeping work for you. You can set up customer accounts, enter sales, create invoices, track late payments, and

monitor expenses and bank accounts easily. By keeping your business information in one place you won't have to wade through a pile of paper to see if you invoiced a client or received payments. To find information about software for your business, run an Internet search on bookkeeping or accounting software to compare popular brands.

- **Always keep your personal finances separate from your business finances.**
  This means establishing business checking and savings accounts, using a business credit card for business purchases and documenting personal money loaned to your business. Make sure to record any payments back to yourself so that your accounts are kept balanced.

- **Save all business-related receipts in an easy-to-remember location.**
  A file folder, storage cabinet, even a shoebox will work. Include anything related to travel, office equipment and supplies, transportation, software, and any other business-related purchases you make. If you use your personal car, computer equipment, and phone for business purposes make sure to keep all receipts relating to the business use of those items. If your business makes charitable donations keep those

receipts as well. You will need your receipts when tax time rolls around to figure out your tax deductions.

Spend time up-front establishing proper and accurate bookkeeping procedures so you can spend the rest of your time managing your profits rather than counting your losses.

Example: Taking the sin out of Sin City

The bright lights and seemingly endless potential for prosperity drew one budding entrepreneur to Sin City. Lynn, a talented singer and model, moved to Las Vegas to pursue an entertainment career—but ended up as a business owner.

She came to Las Vegas from Illinois on a greyhound bus. But there were no coughing seatmates or screaming babies on her bus. This bus was a fully renovated, single owner, traveling bus perfect for making the trip to the good life.

The bus proved to be more than funky transportation. After Lynn and a fellow traveler arrived in Las Vegas, they found that while the bus was a comfortable ride, it was also expensive to store. Starting over in a new city meant expenses—and paying storage costs for an unwieldy vehicle wasn't in the budget.

Lynn and her friend started asking around to see if anyone was in the market for a bus, and to their surprise they got a taker. A Las Vegas band was looking for a bus to transport themselves and their equipment to gigs. Lynn and her friend made the sale.

They also made friends with the band members and discovered that they needed models for an upcoming photo shoot. Lynn had some contacts in the local modeling scene and offered her expertise. The band jumped at the chance for help and became Lynn's first client in her unintended foray into business ownership.

As often happens with new businesses, Lynn's business was born before the business plan was conceived. Lynn completed her assignment for the band then sat down to plot out a course of action.

Lynn had always been drawn to the entertainment industry. She came to Las Vegas planning to work as a singer in a Vegas show. But when working on the band's project, Lynn saw a different opportunity.

While interviewing models for the band's photo shoot, Lynn heard stories about shady agents who preyed on the young women. Lynn saw a chance to help up-and-comers steer clear of the entertainment underworld while also showcasing their talents through local promotional opportunities.

Once Lynn defined the services she would offer, she focused on the financial aspects of starting her business. Because she had just moved to town and had a limited budget, she had to be thrifty when setting up her business. She identified the following expenses:

- office rental
- office equipment including a computer, printer, and fax
- new cell phone plan to account for increased call volume
- Internet service since many of her bookings would be arranged online.

- accounting software to manage the business finances
- liability insurance to protect her personal assets if she was hit with a lawsuit.
- marketing costs associated with the promotional services she offered to bands and models.

After identifying expenses, Lynn cringed. She knew she couldn't fund her business solely out-of-pocket. She reviewed her expenses to see if she could do some trimming. One unnecessary expense was office rent. She could operate her business easily from home thus avoiding office rental costs.

Working from home also would provide her with flexibility so she could pursue other part-time work to pay household bills until her business got off the ground. She could limit marketing efforts to online tools such as social networking sites and e-mail to reduce those costs.

But she still had a shortfall in her budget. She would self-fund the expenses that were within her reach based on a part-time income, which as a newcomer to Las Vegas had yet to materialize. But Lynn was determined to give her business a go.

She hit the hot Las Vegas pavement to search for investors. She found businesses willing to barter for services. For example, a club would provide a venue for a band at no cost if she would market the event to bring in bar revenue. Bartering was a short-term solution—one that would need to be phased out if Lynn wanted to turn a profit.

She also found several small entertainment businesses that were interested in her efforts and offered start-up investments in exchange for a first glimpse at the entertainers Lynn promoted. The remaining funds would come from her clients.

The problem

As soon as Lynn had some initial start-up capital, she began taking on clients. She had yet to find a part-time job but figured that some quick income from her business would help her make ends meet. She quickly discovered that in the entertainment industry sometimes there's more give than take, especially when an entertainer is just starting out.

Collecting client payments proved challenging. Young models and bands fresh out of their garages spoke a good game, but when it came down to paying for Lynn's services, they handed her excuses not dollars. Also, bartering for services became the norm not the exception and Lynn saw no profits in her coffers. After being in business for a few short months, Lynn ran out of money.

The solution

Lynn wasn't ready to hop the next bus out of Vegas just yet, but she decided to hold her business plans until she had a steady income stream. She put a hold on new clients and made searching for a part-time job her full-time job.

She also developed strict guidelines for when she would barter for services. She limited the practice to low-cost items that didn't add much to her bottom line. She also drew up client contracts that required partial payments before services were provided. With these changes, Lynn had a better chance of earning revenue to cover business expenses and eventually turn a profit.

A couple months later she found a part-time job and also re-launched her business with a promotional party for another local band whose star was rising. The band parked their bus in front of the music venue, unloaded their gear and handed Lynn a check. Lynn was back in business and the Las Vegas lights shined a little brighter that night.

Chapter 5:
Making work-from-home work for you

Home is where the heart is, as the saying goes. And for many new business owners, home is where the office is. For the entrepreneur with confectionery talent and chocolate dreams, the family kitchen makes a superb test kitchen. The aspiring game developer codes away the evening hours listening to music in the basement computer room. The inventor cuts and welds metal into exotic shapes in a backyard workshop.

Working from home may seem like the ideal situation. Home is inspiring, relaxing and comforting. The commute to your office is measured in footsteps, not miles, and the length of your workday is yours to define. But working from home comes with hazards.

A year into my adventure as a business owner, I was awaiting a video call from my flagship client. He had a project for me and wanted to discuss the details. I was delighted. I holed up in the quiet space of my basement office waiting to join the video meeting.

I was nervous about how I was going to manage my two young children who were peacefully playing the living room next door. The angelic beauties appeared sedate, stacking blocks in their play space.

But mayhem was lurking. Little did I know that putting on my headset was a trigger that awakens the devious imps that live inside children. I was about to experience the rise of these netherworld creatures.

The client joined the meeting and I put on my headset to start the conversation. I talked with my client about the details of his project, unaware of the stirrings in the room next door. Soon, I noticed two sets of eyes peering into my office. The little ones had moved their play space to the hallway outside my office and had a direct view to my computer screen.

As my client explained his project, my children toddled through my office door and smiled sweetly. Then they released the imps. My youngest wailed in decibels sure to crack glass. She scratched at my knees with her baby claws and gnawed on my ankles with her razor teeth. My oldest jumped up into an office chair and spun around until she slipped off knocking her noggin on the chair leg. Then she joined in the wailing.

The phone went silent as the noise became deafening. I put my hand over the phone and shouted, "That's enough!"

But it was too late. My client politely said, "It sounds like I reached you at a bad time. I'll call back later."

He never did. But I did call him several days later and made assurances I would better manage my work-from-home situation. Luckily, I was able to mend the relationship. After that experience, I am now wise to the ways of imps and the risks of the home office. So, before you trade in your business suits for sweatpants, consider these truths:

With kids at home, you need childcare

If your kids take consistent naps and you can fit your work into naptime—great! Otherwise, make plans for childcare. Trying to take a phone call or work on a client's project with a screaming child in the background is just plain miserable. Believe me, I've tried. It's frustrating to have to place a client on hold to calm a crying baby or wipe burp-up off your computer keyboard.

If you have a neighbor or relative that is willing and able to pop over when you need quiet time to work, call them. If you can schedule your phone calls ahead of time, work around your babysitter's schedule. If you can't schedule calls, give your babysitter a heads up about the time you will be working and ask him or her to be available during that time.

Having a list of daycare centers or providers who provide back-up care is also valuable in case you need to run to a meeting and your babysitter is not available. Your children will likely enjoy the break from the usual routine, you'll get quality work time, and your customers will get the professional service they deserve.

Working at home requires discipline

Breathing exhaust fumes while you crawl along in rush hour traffic is no fun. Neither is worrying about whether your boss noticed you were fifteen minutes late for work because you were stuck in traffic. Working from home has definite advantages over working in an office, but it also poses unique challenges.

At home, you are your only boss and co-worker. You have to rely on yourself to find solutions to day-to-day work issues and to complete your work on time. With no supervisor to provide feedback about your projects, it's up to you to make sure you are producing quality work. You are the direct line to your customers so all problems start and end with you.

Having a network of experts to help you out is a must. These may be friends, consultants, professional organizations, past coworkers, even family. Use them when needed; but remember, when you own the business, you also own the responsibilities that come with it.

You are the boss—sort of

You are never truly your own boss—whether working at an office or when working from home. Your customers and clients are your boss. In an office environment the layers of personnel make it easy to forget who you really work for.

Yes, you report to a supervisor, manager, or board, but you serve your customers and clients.

This fact becomes more apparent when you are your customers' only point of contact. Golf on a Monday afternoon may sound good to you, but guess what? Your client needs his or her project finished as soon as possible. Better reschedule the golf game. Also, get cozy with your PDA, cell phone, voicemail system, and e-mail. These will become a lifeline to your clients.

Take note: Your customers may be your boss, but they shouldn't own all your time. To avoid working night and day, set aside work time and leisure time. Businesses provide vacation time for their employees. You can do the same for yourself. Notify your clients of your business hours and planned vacation times. Offer them an alternative for reaching you when you are out of the office such as leaving a voicemail message that you can answer during regular business hours. Then turn off your cell phone and take a break. After all, you are the boss.

Pajamas are not the new business suit

You can wear your pajamas to the office when you work out of your house. But do you really want to? When was the last time you went to a meeting with someone wearing slippers and a stinky robe? Whether you work in an office or work at home, you are a professional. Establishing a "dress code" will help you maintain your sense of professionalism.

While three-piece suits might be overkill when typing away in your home office, a nice pair of jeans and a sweater would be appropriate. If clients are visiting you consider wearing dress pants and a dress shirt or blouse. Your style of dress is ultimately driven by the type of business you are performing. But what you wear should be a conscious decision, not an afterthought. You don't want a client who happens to be in your neighborhood catching you in your polka dot pajamas and fuzzy slippers.

Distractions are distracting

We already covered whining kids, but what about dishes, laundry, dust bunnies, and the Internet. If you are a neat freak like me chances are you'll have a difficult time putting down the broom to pick up a client's telephone call. And it's really easy to get caught up in the daily happenings on the Internet. Working at home requires a good deal of self-control and motivation to be successful.

To avoid distractions, schedule time for work when you are most productive. If you are awake and focused you are less likely to stray from your work. Creating an office space away from the hub of your house also helps. I work at the kitchen table while my children are away or quietly playing elsewhere, but I do use my downstairs office when the household is busy.

If your workspace has a door, make sure to shut it. A closed door will encourage you to stay at your desk. Also, keep a calendar with project deadlines in plain sight so you always know where to focus your energy. Consider using a PDA or software that can warn you of impending deadlines. An annoying beep or pop-up is a great way to stay on task. Finally, give yourself some slack time. Everyone needs rest.

Using coworking spaces

Consider a co-working office if you are prone to distractions at home. Co-working spaces are shared offices available for rent by individuals or small teams. These spaces have business equipment, private or shared desk space, conference rooms, and other office amenities without a long-term rental commitment. The space is ideal for meeting with clients or taking client calls, or for hosting networking events when a professional setting is needed.

Most co-working spaces can be rented by the day, week, or month. Co-working spaces are often more affordable than renting an office space with a long-term lease because you don't need to pay utilities and maintenance on your own. You share those costs with others.

When working in a co-working space, you will be surrounded by a community of other professionals which can help with networking, sharing ideas, and possibly even providing business leads.

A co-working space creates structure and separates your work life from your home life. While in the co-working space, you can focus on building your business, then, when you head home you can unplug and relax.

Success will not happen overnight

Just because you were a whiz kid in the workplace doesn't mean you'll find instant success out on your own. Running a business requires a commitment of time and resources and a high level of product and industry knowledge. On average it takes new businesses three years to become profitable. Many never become profitable, but those that do provide their owners with earning power and the pride that comes from succeeding at something they love. Business success can be attributed to hard work, dedication, good timing, and a bit of luck. Some elements of success are controllable, some are not.

Expect long hours. Depending on your work background, you may be used to long hours and 24/7 problem solving. If you came from a strict nine-to-five working environment, be prepared for a lifestyle change. When you manage your time wisely you can focus on opportunities to grow your business.

Expect the unexpected. During your previous career experiences, you developed a skill set and an awareness of business practices—some good and some not so good. Use what you know to tackle the challenges that confront you. If you set yourself up for success from the start, you'll have a better chance of achieving your goals.

Organization will save your organization

In the office, you had a small corner of the corporate world from which to ply your trade. You may have had a cubby in cubicle city or an office with a window. Either way, your space was compact, standardized, and vacuumed by the night cleaning crew. Not so at home.

Unless you live in a studio apartment, your home has multiple rooms to spread out your stuff. And stuff can make a mess. Receipts, contact lists, and paperwork all pile up quickly. Mix in your personal bills, magazines, and junk mail and you have business paper chaos.

Searching through stacks of paperwork reduces productivity. Missing documents can lead to errors. As a result, customers may be dissatisfied with your service and may look to fulfill their business needs elsewhere. Organization isn't complicated. It just requires a little extra effort and a method to sort through the madness.

The first step is to set aside space for a filing cabinet or two. In today's electronic business world much is done through e-mail, text and phone, but paper still exists and needs to be stored. Create a file for bills, customer documents, receipts and any other documents you frequently receive. You may need these documents for backup if questions arise about work you have performed or bills that require payment.

Note that receipts worth saving include your personal phone bills, credit card bills, business purchases, gas and mileage and any other receipts associated with your business. Many of these items are deductible at tax time and the amounts will be based on the receipts you have saved.

Next, set up a filing system for your computer. This filing system can mirror your paper filing system if you like consistency and will be scanning in paper documents for backup. Otherwise, choose categories that make the most sense. This could include folders for each client to save invoices, receipts, client work in progress, important e-mail messages, and documents.

Consider purchasing contact management software. Losing contact information is a quick way to miss business opportunities. Having to call a client to get their address is embarrassing the first time. The next time it's just unprofessional. Contact management software provides a single location to store all your contact information, client conversation notes, reminders, and even documents such as letters that you want to associate with a particular customer.

Before purchasing the software, consider whether you will actually use it. It takes commitment to add every note and every letter to a customer entry. If you don't need to do this, an Excel file or Word document can work well to store contact information if you manage it carefully.

Example: Pajama time

It's 8 a.m. Rick's alarm beeped on his bed stand. He stretched, scratched his back, and covered his eyes to block the sun streaming in under his blinds. Time for work. He put on his bathrobe and walked down the stairs to shower and shave. His routine usually started at 7 a.m., but he was out entertaining clients the previous night and needed to sleep off the good karma. He tripped over the threshold to the bathroom door and caught his robe sleeve on the doorknob.

"Darn doorknob," he said freeing his sleeve. He heard snickering and realized he was not alone. Watching his morning folly were two employees and an office dog named fluffy.

Rick was stinky, groggy, and thoroughly embarrassed.

The problem

Rick owned a graphic design studio. His office was a large patio off the back of his house. It had a separate entrance but was connected to the home's only bathroom by a shared door. Two designers worked out of the office and usually arrived between 8 a.m. and 8:30 a.m. A third employee who performed administrative tasks worked out of her home.

Rick launched his business in the early 1990s and was heavily influenced by the dot com emphasis on frivolity and flexibility in the workplace. He said pooh pooh to structure in his day and lived for business lunches and martini dinners. He was an idea man who wanted to take the world by storm.

The design business was small but had growth potential. Rick had a string of prospects and current clients ran the gamut from technology companies to government-funded community groups. The designers created client websites, brochures, ads and anything else Rick could entice clients to send his way. Rick led the team by sharing design ideas and meeting with prospects and clients.

While Rick had design talent and a penchant for sales, he lacked organization and time management skills. Out of practicality, his employees kept regular work hours and didn't buy into the free flow business style Rick envisioned. They came to work, completed their projects, and went home to their families.

But Rick came to the office when the spirit of design—or his wife—moved him. Often, he would lounge around his home until mid-morning while his employees spun around in their office chairs waiting for work direction. Occasionally he would treat his employees to the pajama fashion show which no-one wanted front row seats to see.

Rick's designer dreams came crashing down on a cold winter day as a project deadline came due. A large client had hired the company to build a website for an upcoming trade show. Rick was the point of contact between the company and the design firm. He discussed the project requirements with the company and promised them his best work.

However, he failed to relate the project requirements, timeline, and other pertinent project goals to his design team. He assigned pieces of the project to the team and they got to work. Over the next few days, Rick made occasional appearances in the office. In his absence the team completed their work then sat and waited, sat and waited. With no additional work direction, they called it an early day on Friday and left for the weekend.

On Monday, Rick was in the office bright and early. The client called Friday afternoon after the employees had left for the weekend. The company was expecting good news about their completed project due that Friday and instead got an answering machine. Perhaps the answering machine saved them from the headache of learning that their project was in shambles.

Parts were done but were not in line with the client's expectations. The entirety of the project needed to be completed, reviewed, and finalized. Rick was in the hot seat. After listening to the reminder message on his answering machine, he spent his weekend struggling at his computer to finish the project. By Monday, he was ready to place blame. Before he had the chance, his employees did it for him by quitting their positions. Left without employees and with a project to finish by himself, Rick wondered what went wrong.

Lessons learned

Rick had vision, ambition, and talent. But he had overlooked key success factors necessary to manage his business.

Rick was carefree and creative but he lacked discipline. When he worked for an employer, those traits served him well. His supervisors managed his day while he designed beautiful communications pieces that impressed clients. When he launched his own company and stepped into the manager's role, he had difficulty making the switch from employee to employer. His random work style frustrated his employees and led to confusion about work responsibilities which led to missed deadlines.

Being an employer takes discipline. Like employees, employers need clearly defined boundaries, responsibilities, and expectations. Employers are leaders, and successful leaders hold themselves to high standards. When an employer is conscientious about his work, employees will follow suit.

He also lacked professionalism. Showing up at the office in pajamas is unprofessional, even if the office is your porch. Appearances guide perceptions. Each time an employee snickers about your wardrobe choice, you lose a tad more respect. When you work from home, it's important to make the mental switch from homebody to business owner once you walk into your workspace. This is true even if you don't have employees. Wearing clothes appropriate to the workplace not only boosts your sense of professionalism, it also can increase your motivation level. When you look like a business owner you are more likely to act like one.

Before Rick incorporated his business and hired employees, he honed his skills as a freelance designer for a few months. He enjoyed working on projects late at night and meeting with his clients for an hour or so during the day. He stored project information in his head and abhorred timelines. He enjoyed the adrenaline rush of marathon design sessions the day before a deadline.

But hiring employees changes everything. Project timelines and requirements must be clearly defined and communicated effectively. Using project management techniques such as identifying tasks, setting timelines, and tracking project milestones is an ideal way to keep a project on schedule. Touching base with employees at a scheduled time or on a daily basis is key to identifying project issues before they bury your project in misunderstandings and confusion. Organization is about knowing what needs to be done and when and having a well-defined plan to achieve the desired outcome.

The conclusion

After his employees took their leave, Rick did some soul-searching. His strength was his design talent. His shortcomings were his lack of discipline and organization. He realized that he had taken on the responsibility of managing employees too quickly. He decided to reassess whether he was really prepared to be master of his domain by returning to freelancing. He would hone his organization and planning skills until he was better able to lead others.

Chapter 6:
All the toys

My little one knows no limits when it comes to her wants. Half a bowl of oatmeal at breakfast isn't enough. She wants all the oatmeal. At snack time, she won't settle for a handful of raspberries. She demands all the raspberries. Her child's mind can't yet comprehend that sometimes a handful of raspberries is all it takes to fill her belly.

Teaching the importance of restraint to a three-year-old is an important life lesson, though, since it will lay the groundwork for her well-being as an adult.

Restraint is also an important concept when managing a business. In the excitement of pursuing a dream, it's easy to get caught up in seeking big gains and quick returns without focusing on the long-term health of the company. Rapid growth, overspending and lack of direction are pitfalls that can spell doom for even high potential businesses.

Goal setting

Goals are the written or verbal pronouncements that provide a framework for your ambition. Goals are written as complete sentences and are specific, measurable, attainable, and realistic. A timeline for achieving the goal is also an important factor. For example, the goal "To sell handbags across America" is better written as "My goal is to sell handbags in every major department store in all 50 states by 2012."

Goals are generally split into short-term and long-term goals. Short-term goals are those to strive for during your first three years in business. After three years, goals are long-term.

Example

- Short-term: I will launch my business in my hometown within three months.
- Long-term: I will sell my business for $300,000 within seven to 10 years.

Within the short-term and long-term categories you can include small goals and large goals.

Example

- Small: I will make $500 in sales for my first three months.
- Large: I will expand my service to nine states in one year.

One way to develop goals is to brainstorm a list of goals you hope to achieve. Write down every dream, every plan, and every wish no matter how simple or outlandish. Then organize your goals into four lists:

- small short-term goals
- large short-term goals
- small long-term goals
- large long-term goals

Pick two or three from the list that fit best with your business plan and vision for your business. The goals you select should be measurable, attainable, realistic and have a definite timeline for completion.

After you have identified your goals, the next step is to create a plan to meet them. Developing a plan to meet goals is really the same process you go through to plan any project. First you identify the tasks that need to be completed to reach the goal. Start broad. Then break each task down into smaller pieces if needed. For example, if you choose the goal stating that "the local newspaper will feature my handbags my first month in business," the task breakdown might include the following:

- Search the newspaper or online news site to find the section most suited for a handbag feature
- Identify the media contact for that section
- Write a press release announcing the launch of the handbag line
- Send a press release to the media contact
- Follow up with a phone call to the media contact

Once you have your task list, develop a timeline for completing each task. Keep your goal's end date in mind.

The timeline for the handbag example may look like this:

- Search the newspaper to find the section most suited for a handbag feature—three days
- Identify the media contact for that section—one day
- Write a press release announcing the launch of the handbag line—three days
- Send a press release to the media contact—one day
- Follow up with a call to the media contact—two weeks

Now, determine resources you will need to complete the tasks. If you need additional staff and funding, plan how to meet those needs. For our handbag example, you may need someone to write a press release if you are not comfortable doing so. This will require a financial outlay to pay a consultant's rate. Don't forget to include your time as a resource. Schedule the tasks related to your goal into your daily schedule as you would any other meeting or project.

After the details of your plan are finalized, put it in action. Because setting a goal is not the ultimate end. Reaching it is.

Evaluating opportunities

When you write your goals, your mind may race in exciting directions. You see visions of your product advertised on the side of buses and celebrities hawking your services on national television. You might think—expand, expand, expand—and you envision more products, a dozen new service offerings, even a totally new direction.

It's easy to think big when you are launching a business. It's also easy to quickly lose sight of why you went into business in the first place. You started your business to do what you love and know well. You may be an expert at the service you provide. The process you use to deliver a product to customers may be more efficient than your competitors. Your special expertise is your core competency.

Focus drives businesses to success. But focus is lost when you lose sight of your core competencies. New opportunities are important to the health of your business. These may include partnership and affiliate possibilities, new product lines, complementary product lines, and new market options. Pursuing the right opportunities can add to your bottom line, but focusing on the wrong opportunities is distracting.

If you find that you are jumping at every interesting opportunity whether or not it suits your business goals, you need to step back. First, evaluate how you are using your resources. Are you spending enough time and financial resources on developing your core competencies or are you finding yourself going off on tangents. If you determine your days are muddled with projects and decisions not relating to your core business, you need to bring your focus in line with your business goals.

Your next step is to make a list of opportunities that peak your interest and establish criteria to judge whether these opportunities have value to your business. Some basic questions to ask include:

- Is the opportunity profitable?
- Does the opportunity help me meet my business objectives?
- Does the opportunity fit with the vision I have defined for my company?
- Do I have the resources to take advantage of the opportunity and still operate my business effectively?
- Do I have the expertise to incorporate this opportunity into my business plan?
- Is this an opportunity that will appeal to my customers?

This stage doesn't require in-depth research. A cursory search of information related to the opportunity will provide enough background to determine whether the opportunity has potential and fits within your business goals. Based on your answer, rank opportunities on a one-to-10 scale, one being the least likely to benefit your company and 10 being a good fit for your business.

Opportunities with a 10 rating deserve more in-depth research. Apply enough resources (time, money, and staff) to analyze the opportunities without impacting your daily business operations. Your research may include online information gathering, meetings with other companies and financial analysis to determine the opportunity's profit potential. You will also need to plan the steps involved to take advantage of the opportunity.

If your analysis finds that an opportunity fits within your budget, has profit potential, and is doable with the resources you have available, go for it. But remember, there are no guarantees. Even after careful analysis, an opportunity you pursue can fizzle. Risk is a part of business, but with great risks come great rewards.

Managing growth

When starting a business, it's tempting to want to leap to the top of the pack right away. You are throwing your money, time, and energy into your business, why shouldn't it grow rapidly? More customers means more money, which means instant success. Right? Not always. Growing too rapidly can drain your pocketbook and time, leaving your customers to suffer the consequences. Slow growth, on the other hand, has many advantages.

Creating a positive customer experience

When you add customers slowly you can focus on providing a positive customer experience. This is especially true of service-oriented businesses. Customers have an expectation of the level of care you will provide throughout the sales process and on an ongoing basis.

For example, I build websites for commercial businesses. I meet with the client to work out the website structure and gather content for the site. I help the client through technical issues during the site's development. And finally, I help launch the site. But my relationship with the client doesn't end on the day the website is launched. I am available after launch to address any issues that come up, to update content when needed, and to add design elements not built into the initial site. It would be hard for me to provide for customers' needs if I was spending all my time chasing down leads. Slow growth helps provide a way to balance customer acquisition with devoting time to your current customers.

Choosing your customers

Building your customer base slowly also can lead to higher quality customers. A high-quality customer is one that purchases your products and services on a regular basis, pays their bills on time, and advocates for your business when given the opportunity. Depending on the type of business you own, you may be able to choose your customers at the same time they are choosing you. How do you do this?

You get to know your customers. You talk with them about what they hope to achieve with your product or service, answer their questions in a timely manner, follow-up after the sale, and keep in contact through e-mail, newsletters, or the telephone. If you don't see your customers face-to-face as is common with Internet-based companies, a friendly thank-you note that encourages feedback may be enough to gain insight into your customer base.

When you identify high-quality customers, focus your attention on providing the best customer service possible. You can do this because you have a small customer base. Your energy isn't being drained by hundreds of customers that are providing minimal returns for your business. Focusing on high-quality customers doesn't mean abandoning one-time customers or providing lesser service to smaller customers. These customers are important to the success of your business and should receive a high-level of customer service as well.

Your goal in focusing on high-quality customers is to expend most of your resources where they will receive the greatest return. You can then apply the remaining resources to ensuring a great experience for all your customers.

One word of caution—growing your customer base too slowly can be hazardous to your financial health. If you have one large client that generates 90 percent of your work, you will be in rough shape if that client leaves. You need to find a happy medium between being selective with your customers and taking on enough business to sustain you financially.

Testing your market

You have researched your market while writing your business plan. You know the market size and trends, where your customers are located, and how they make purchasing decisions. But markets can be fickle. All the research in the world won't help you if a market is disrupted due to economic, environmental, and political conditions or if customers veer in a new direction.

By entering the market slowly, you can test the results of your research and your market assumptions without taking on huge losses if you were wrong. You will also be somewhat shielded from abrupt changes in your customer base. You may take losses when your customers change their buying habits, but your losses will be limited because you didn't exhaust your resources making a large initial plunge into the market.

Financial restraint

With business savvy and a bit of luck, you will start seeing extra zeros in your business bank account. But don't put the down payment on the yacht just yet. Most businesses take at least three years to be profitable.

Unless you have a high-margin product or service, meaning you earn a high proportion of profits based on what you have invested into producing the product, your profits will likely grow slowly until your business is established. But you have business bills to pay and payroll to meet. It is also likely that you will want to reinvest your assets into your business to keep expanding and meeting the needs of your customers. If you are a natural born saver—good for you. If not, here are some tips to help develop your thrifty side:

Do the work yourself—It is tempting to outsource mundane tasks like stuffing envelopes, filing paperwork, and updating your website. If you have time in the day to do these tasks, then do so. Not only will you be able to apply your earnings towards your profit-generating business functions, you will get a great education in the nuts and bolts aspects of running a business. You can hire help as your business grows and you have the income to support additional staff.

Negotiate deals for supplies and services—Building relationships with vendors is a sure way to save money. When a supplier knows you, knows your business, and can expect work from you to come his or her way, he or she will often negotiate rates. For example, if you print marketing materials on a regular basis, working with one trusted print shop will often garner great cost savings.

Having a list of two or three vendors you have worked with or who were recommended by business associates is a good starting point. Talk with the vendors, explain your needs and your anticipated purchasing frequency and see what discounts and pricing the vendor is willing to offer. Make sure you have a general idea of pricing before beginning negotiations or a "good deal" may not actually be a good deal. Always have a backup vendor available in case of rate hikes or if your relationship with your vendor sours.

If you don't need it, don't buy it—This is as true for business spending as it is for personal spending. When launching your business, you may want to buy all the office equipment, software, and furnishings you may ever need to operate your business. And only the best will do. But practice restraint. Make a list of what you truly need during the launch phase. Then shop around. Look for the best price and check for durability. Cheap isn't cost-effective if you have to replace the item several times. But save the $500 office chair for the more financially stable future.

Knowing your personal limits

Expect long hours and sleepless nights when starting a business. But don't overdo it. You need to be at your best and brightest to pull off the exciting venture you are undertaking.

To keep your mind alert and your faculties sharp—manage your time, don't let your business manage you.

First, develop a schedule and stick to it. When you worked for an employer, you arrived at the office in the morning and went home in the afternoon. You may have put in some late nights, but you probably never camped out on the office floor. As your own boss, you may feel obligated to work 24/7. Don't.

Establish office hours and make them clear to your customers. Post your hours on your website and your voice mail. Politely tell customers when they can contact you with questions. Provide some leeway for administrative tasks. If you prefer to do your bookkeeping in the morning, start your workday at 8 a.m. and open for business at 9 a.m. If you like to work in the afternoon, close shop at 5 p.m. and finish up the day's paperwork by 6 p.m. When you develop a schedule and stick to it, midnight runs to a local print shop will be the exception not the norm.

Second, make time for family and friends. They need you. You need them. They will keep you sane. It's that simple. But it takes effort to balance your family-life with your business. It's easy to get caught up in the daily workings of your business and forget to make time for connecting with the important people in your life. But those connections are important to your health and well-being. Plan outings with your family and friends and make a point not to talk business. Be leisurely and enjoy being entertained. Easy, right?

When you own a new business, relaxing doesn't always come easy. Your mind will churn through your lists of to do's while you're trying to enjoy your child's music recital. You'll be planning how to make the next big sale, while your friends are ordering another round of chicken wings. Nurturing your relationships takes commitment, but as a business owner you understand commitment. You are committed to building your business. You are committed to finding success. Just add commitment to friends and family into the mix and you will achieve the business owner's nirvana.

Third, know when to call for help. Those same family members and friends that make your days more enjoyable can also provide valuable help in a pinch. Recruit your computer-savvy kids to create ads and enter data into your customer database. Drag a friend along to a trade show in exchange for tickets to a game or a gift certificate to a favorite restaurant. If you know a college student looking for career experience, invite him to work in your office during busy times. Your friends and family may enjoy learning about your business and you'll get the help you need during challenging times.

Example: Breaking up is hard to do

A greenhouse client of mine prided himself on his customer service focus. His business sold direct to customers and made every face-to-face meeting count. The resident plant expert talked with each client about their upcoming projects and offered advice when asked. He made notes about what plants customers requested most often so he was sure to grow enough inventory to accommodate the customers' needs. The business also had a quality guarantee for every product sold that stated that the plants would be replaced within 30 days of purchase if they failed to thrive. Finally, the business offered something rare in the greenhouse industry—delivery.

The goal of these customer initiatives was to create a positive customer experience to encourage repeat business. It worked, quickly leading to repeat customers and new customers who had heard about the company through satisfied acquaintances. All was proceeding according to plan. The business was growing, customers were happy, and the bumps in the road were few. Then Carlee happened.

The problem

Carlee was a new customer who learned about the greenhouse through a local gardening organization. She attended a seminar about "green" gardening and with rake and hoe in hand found a corner of her backyard perfectly suited for such a garden. The spot had nutrient-rich black dirt, partial shade, and was low so it collected rainwater. All she needed was the right plants.

Carlee contacted the greenhouse through e-mail. She sent a list of plants and an address for delivery. As was his process, the greenhouse owner sent a confirmation to Carlee with the total cost. Carlee agreed to the amount and the greenhouse owner merrily plucked plants off the shelves and plunked them into the delivery truck.

Then the phone rang. It was Carlee. She had a change in the order. Instead of four Butterfly Milkweed plants, she wanted three Golden Alexanders. And the Prairie Smoke wouldn't do. Instead, she'd like four New England Asters.

"All righty," said the greenhouse owner and he hurriedly removed the original plants from his truck and replaced them with the new order. He slammed the gate on the truck and drove off to deliver the order.

Forty minute later he arrived at Carlee's home to drop off the plants. She was out for the day. He unloaded the pots and placed them neatly on her front porch. He tucked the invoice between her screen door and headed off to make his remaining deliveries. When he arrived home at the end of his workday, he saw the flash of his telephone message light. He checked the message. It was Carlee.

"The plants are all bad," she said frantically. "They have no roots. They all need to be replaced. Call me."

He was befuddled. The plants were fine when they came off the truck. He was frustrated but took a deep breath and called Carlee to set things right. On the phone, she repeated her plant observations.

"The roots are missing. The plants are no good. Please replace them and deliver the new plants tomorrow."

"Fine," he said. "I'll stop by and take a look." But he was thinking, "I've had it with this customer. I'm going to tell her I can't serve her and point her to someone else."

He was ready to say goodbye.

Lessons learned

The greenhouse owner had two choices in moving forward in his relationship with the challenging customer. He could do everything possible to keep the customer happy, or he could cut and run. He could refuse to replace the plants and point the customer to another greenhouse that would serve her needs.

The owner thought long and hard. When developing the vision for his business he placed high value on customer service. One of his goals was to be respected in his industry by his customers and peers. But focusing on customer service isn't easy, as the greenhouse owner found. Customers expect much from the businesses they traffic. Some will take advantage of a business's good graces; others will merely hold the business responsible for honoring its policies. The greenhouse had a plant replacement and free delivery policy and Carlee took full advantage.

But was she being unreasonable? The greenhouse owner knew that to be taken seriously as a customer focused business, he needed to honor his customer service policies. So, he did just that. He paid Carlee a visit to talk about her gardening issues. After a short discussion and tour of Carlee's flower beds, he discovered that the problem was not with the plants. The problem was with Carlee's inexperience as a gardener. Carlee expected the plants to behave and look a certain way based on the simple flower garden she planted the year before. However, the plants from the greenhouse were different from common varieties found at the big box stores where Carlee purchased last year's plants. They bloomed at a different point during the season and the root structure was shorter than that of the plants Carlee was familiar with.

The greenhouse owner breathed a sigh of relief. The cause of Carlee's frustration was a simple misunderstanding, and one that he could fix with a bit of horticulture briefing. Problem solved without losing a customer. In fact, because of the greenhouse owner's response to her gardening questions, Carlee passed his name along to her local garden club and he received three more orders.

While disaster was averted, the greenhouse owner realized he needed a plan for dealing with problem customers. Since he worked with landscapers, developers, government groups, and individual consumers larger conflicts were inevitable.

He sat down with a pen and paper and wrote out a list of reasons to turn customers away. He came up with the following:

- Refusal to pay past invoices
- Showing aggressive or abusive language or behavior towards himself or his employees

- Repeatedly requesting a refund or replacement plants when the plant damage was caused by a factor not covered in the refund policy (e.g., mowing over the plants.)
- Threats to harm the company's reputation if it doesn't provide a non-standard discount or pricing scheme.

If additional conflicts related to pricing, delivery, plant quality, and service arose, he would work closely with customers to resolve the issues quickly and in a friendly manner to achieve a positive outcome.

He knew that focusing on the customer would have its struggles, but ultimately it would create an exceptional buying experience for his customers and differentiate his business as a customer service leader in the industry.

Chapter 7:
Communication matters

As a business owner, you are a communicator. Every day you make choices about what words, images, and body language you use, how you use them, and what message they send about your company.

You communicate when you take customer orders and respond to questions. You communicate when you send an e-mail to a vendor or ask for information from a prospective client. You communicate when you give a presentation to explain your business ideas to investors. Because sending the right message can "make the sale," it is essential to have well-honed communication skills when starting a business.

Large and mid-sized organizations often have communications, marketing, or advertising departments to develop and manage communications projects for a company. While it is beneficial to have communications experts creating communications that define the company, a company's reputation is created by every employee in the organization not just a specific department or team.

In a small business, this concept is especially important because a variety of responsibilities fall to one or a few people. Small businesses often don't have the advantage of handing off the communications development portion of the business to a department dedicated to crafting messages.

Don't panic if you are not a strong presenter, talker or writer. Improving everyday communication is easy if you follow some simple steps.

Talk, write, be heard

When you communicate you are on a stage and your audience is the different groups of people you are contacting. Employees may expect witty repartee, while shareholders may want the facts and nothing but the facts. Customers may want both depending on the type of product or service you are providing. This is true whether you are sending an e-mail, talking to someone on the phone, or writing a letter.

Craft your message for the audience

Knowing your audience and having a strong sense of your company's image will help you develop a consistent communication style for your company. If your company sells to a hip, free-wheeling clientele and maintains a carefree employee environment, have fun with your communications. Be informal and vivid (but tasteful). If you are a button-down, pin-stripe business reflect that in your communications. Choose formal words that signify strength and stability. If you are still fine-tuning your company's identity, stick to clear, professional language easily understood by all.

Send a consistent message

Many companies develop stylebooks that define company terminology and acronyms and set standards for business communication. This is a simple way to help maintain consistency in the messages you send from your company. If you have a tagline or common phrase you want employees to use in communication materials, list it in the stylebook. Also include any special formatting requirements you want employees to follow for letters, e-mails, and other written communications.

For example, if all e-mails should contain your company's address and phone number, make that clear. If customers should always be greeted by their first name, include that in the style book. If invoices should always include your logo, address, phone number, and website make sure employees know the rules. Even if you are the sole employee of your company, having a list of common communication conventions that you want to follow will be a helpful reminder.

Consistency in your communication shows your audience that you are a solid, well-structured company. Your audience knows what to expect when they do business with you. If their first experience is positive, they know they can expect further communication with you to be positive as well.

Be concise

People are busy. Concise communication is best in most situations. Choosing your words carefully and getting right to the point will open more doors than rambling soliloquies. In face-to-face or phone conversations, some friendly chatter is expected. But make sure to have a list of key points you want to address and stick to the list. Respond to questions with direct answers and include all pertinent information to reduce the need for extensive follow-up conversations. Listening is key. Always carry a small notepad or take notes on your phone and follow-up with any information you don't have on hand.

Written communication should also be direct and short. A two-to three-paragraph format works for most letters and e-mail messages. If you are replying to an e-mail that has a long list of other replies, summarize the e-mail in your reply before hitting send.

If you are requesting something from your reader, make that clear in the first paragraph. Follow with a second paragraph that includes specific details that make your point or that explain the situation. The third paragraph is a closing paragraph that can include next steps, contact information, and any calls to action.

If your prospect, client, or customer prefers texting or using online communication tools, honor their wishes.

Edit, edit, edit

Most communication and e-mail applications have spell check. Use it. Then re-read your written communications several times to make sure you catch spelling and grammar errors that spell check didn't catch. Remove any industry buzzwords or acronyms that are not commonly known. These could confuse people not familiar with your industry.

In e-mails or texts avoid using all caps. People may think you are yelling. Avoid underlining as well. It can be confused with linking conventions on websites. Also, read your messages before sending them to make sure they don't sound angry or condescending. And remember to include greetings and salutations where appropriate. Finally, if a telephone call could help resolve a situation more quickly, pick up the phone.

Listen up

We often ask our children to "open your ears" when they are not paying attention to what we are saying. Sometimes we need to take our own advice. It's easy to get wrapped up in what we are saying to our audience, whether it is employees, clients, or peers. We have ideas to share and points to make. But a key part of good communication is listening. When you are engaged in active listening you will gain valuable insight into your contact's demeanor and business needs.

When talking to a client, employee, or peer, whether in person or on the phone, these tips will help you improve your listening skills:

- Focus your attention on what that person is saying not on other conversations or events around you.
- Clear your mind of clutter; don't try to multi-task while you are engaged in a conversation.
- Let the contact complete his or her thoughts without interruption.
- Take notes about the key details of the conversation, especially if they require a response.
- Repeat or rephrase what the speaker said to make sure you understood their intended point.
- Ask for clarification of unclear discussion points.

By actively listening you can respond to questions promptly in a communication style your contact feels comfortable with.

Make it personal

You can say thank you to your customers in a text message or e-mail, but it lacks the personal touch that says, "I give a darn." And don't we all want to know that when we give something of ourselves someone else gives a darn? This is true for personal relationships and it's true for business. When a customer writes a check for a product or service, a simple handwritten thank-you goes a long way towards creating goodwill.

- If you're a service provider, send a signed thank-you note to first-time customers.
- Write a quick thank-you or greeting on invoices.
- When you receive a big order, send a written acknowledgement.
- Ask your staff to sign greeting cards sent to customers.

Adding a personal touch lets your customers know you're thinking about them. When it comes time for them to make their next purchase, they just might return the sentiment.

Stop with the gobbledygook and speak human

Let me set the stage. You are holding an all-employee meeting online. The agenda is on the screen and leaders are lined up and ready to speak. Cameras are on. Everyone but the speaker is muted. The first presentation starts.

"Welcome everyone. Today we are going to discuss the paradigm shift impacting our ability to leverage low hanging fruit. We're working towards creating synergies to capitalize on the new normal. We are primed to think outside the box and take a holistic approach to add value to our value proposition. Does anyone know the ask? Want to huddle? Ping me and we'll hop on a call."

Computer cameras capture blank stares, empty seats, and a dog licking the computer screen. When the master unmute button is clicked and the presenter asks for feedback or questions, the only sound is silence. Why? Because the words that just fell out of the presenter's mouth mean nothing. Corporate speak dressed in an intellectual cloak is gobbledygook. It is meaningless language designed to impress without imparting real information.

Unfortunately, corporate speak is the language employees hear every day at team meetings, in corporate lectures, and in developmental training. It's common throughout employee-focused news features highlighting big wins and business strategies. The corners of the company website are gummed up with nonsense language that hides as goals and project plans.

A company can't forge ahead when no one understands the directions.

Corporate speak alienates employees and customers

Employees drive company success. They make the wheels turn, but when they have no idea how to put the car in the right gear, the result is a sharp turn into a mud-filled ditch. It's hard to make decisions and act on leaderships direction when that direction isn't clear.

How are employees supposed to leverage opportunities when no one tells them what those opportunities are and what tools are available to grab them? It's hard to think outside the box, when you're not even sure where the box is located.

Also, if an organization has employees with a variety of cultural backgrounds and native languages, using corporate speak will isolate many of those employees. They may not understand what was said or what part they play in the big sweeping statements. Keep wording free of corporate speak and you'll keep your employees' attention.

Don't sound smart, be smart.

Leaders who hide behind corporate speak sometimes do so because they don't understand company strategy. When even the leaders are confused, it's time for decision-makers to go back to the drawing board and start over.

Leaders who get out of the boardroom and talk to front-line employees are more likely to understand the market and its challenges and opportunities. Then, it is possible to craft an understandable strategy that everyone can get on board with. Big words don't make good strategy. If goals are wrapped in corporate speak that are cloaked in grandiose diatribes (big words with a lot of rah rah), the company's leaders have likely lost focus. Good strategy is based on the real time industry needs in the words of those who have the skill and experience to meet those needs.

Reread what you wrote

Leaders should ask themselves, does your writing make sense? Is it possible to identify the key points and are they meaningful? If not, rewrite using plain language. The guideline in journalism and marketing is to write for the audience at a sixth-grade level. The same guidelines should be in place for company communications. By writing in plain language, leaders aren't assuming that the audience can't think beyond a sixth-grade level. They are crafting messages that are clear and communicate the intended meaning.

Here's an example.

- **Corporate speak:** The company will leverage corporate partnerships to realize cost efficiencies
- **Plain language:** We'll work with our business partners to find the lowest costs for materials

Speak so people understand

Remember that most employees don't have access to the boardroom. Don't assume that everyone knows something about everything that goes on in the company. Provide background when talking about corporate projects. Set the scene and tell the story. If you don't know the project's history, bring in the person closest to the project and let them share the details.

Communications shouldn't just come from the top. Information is more understandable when it comes directly from those you live the project day in and day out. Don't re-translate the details into corporate wording. Keep in a human voice.

If you don't know what to say, say nothing at all

Sometimes managers feel like they need to explain something, but they don't have all information need to speak wisely. To compensate, they create circular language that avoids the issue entirely.

It's better to say, we don't have that information right now then to dance around the subject with meaningless wording. Focus on fielding the questions and researching the details. Then share more fully when the timing is right.

Example: Will the audience please stand up

When my native plant greenhouse client launched his business amidst a green marketing craze the business's communications consultant was a bit baffled by how to position the company's product above the fray. TVs, newspapers, magazines and the Internet were overloaded with claims of eco-friendly, green products. Some claims passed the truthfulness test, others were marginally realistic, but many were downright laughable.

The company's products were truly ecologically sound— their greatest benefit being the preservation and promotion of native landscapes. But how to get the message across to consumers weary of boisterous claims left the consultant scratching her head.

The problem

She had several problems when deciding how to craft the company's promotional message:

- The advantages of native plants are often defined in complex scientific terms which may not appeal to the market.
- The market for native plants is growing, but not well-defined. The path to communicate with the market is unclear and research into what messages appeal to the market is limited.
- The communication goal was fuzzy. The marketing director wasn't sure if she should reiterate the value of native plants to those familiar with the advantages or try to sway newcomers to give native plants a try.

The consultant jotted down communication ideas and potential wording for marketing pieces that would appeal to a large, nondescript consumer base. She envisioned the neighborhood gardener standing in line at the local nursery or grocery store when writing the messages. The result was messages that seemed weak and ill-fitting. Finally, in frustration, she shared her concerns with the company owner.

He read through her musings with fresh eyes and wisdom that came with years in the trade.

"The problem is that you're trying to sell to the wrong audience," said the owner. "Our audience is landscapers, city planners, and environmental organizations, not general consumers. We don't want to appeal to the people that spend $50 on perennials at big box stores. We want to sell to people that spend $500 on plants for city parks and office lawns."

"Got it," said the consultant feeling like the word dunce was painted across her face in red paint.

"I'm sure you'll come up with something great," said the owner. "I used to sell plants at garage sales hoping to make my millions by introducing them to suburban gardeners. After I figured out that $10 for eight hours of work wasn't great take-home pay, I thought twice about that strategy and focused on the professionals, not the home gardeners."

The consultant sighed in relief, happy that she still had a job. But she also realized she had a fourth problem to consider. She was unfamiliar with the company's overall strategy and therefore started her communications planning under the faulty assumption that the company sold to the consumer market.

The solution

The consultant realized she needed to address her knowledge gap about company strategy before she could craft promotional messages suited to the company's goals. She understood the owner's position but wanted in-depth information about the company's market.

To find the key industry players and market specifics she read through the company's business plan. She also looked up key customers by reviewing the company's client list. She perused clients' websites and found news articles about large native landscaping projects. She reviewed trade journals to understand the type of information available to the market about native plants. She also gathered competitor's marketing materials to see how they spoke to the market.

After a few days of research, she made discoveries that helped her address the marketing issues she identified. The first issue she identified related to the language appropriate to the audience. Now that general consumers had been removed from the mix, the audience was clear. They were professionals in the landscape/environmental field who were familiar with the benefits of native plants. Therefore, educating them wasn't necessary.

On the other hand, using overly simplified language would be insulting. Creating a message that focused on the benefits of buying from her greenhouse client in a to-the-point tone was ideal.

To solve the second problem—defining the market—the consultant looked at ads in trade journals to identify the main industry players. Those who weren't already clients were added to the prospect list. Those who were clients were tagged in the client database so that messages could be crafted to appeal specifically to their needs.

The consultant then looked at competitors who served the same market. She made a list of communication vehicles they used to reach the audience. She noted that websites featured event updates, discount information, and project photos. Traditional newsletters and e-newsletters contained similar information. Brochures and ads highlighted each company's unique value to their client base and direct mail pieces announced special programs geared towards the audience.

Finally, the consultant addressed the third issue, defining the communication goals. After talking with the owner, the marketer determined that the communication goal was to expand interest in the company's products among landscape professionals. This meant crafting a message for current customers that focused on how the company would continue to serve their needs. It also meant introducing new customers to the company's features that made it unique.

With a head full of research, the communications consultant set to work crafting messages to generate buzz and position the company as a leader in its market.

Chapter 8:
You are a marketer

Marketing is the process used to get your message and product to your customers and potential customers as effectively as possible. If you've ever had to go door to door with your child selling candy bars for a school fundraiser, you understand marketing basics. The school has probably identified a sales target for you and your fellow candy bar salespeople. Your job is to find the most effective way to reach the target. You want to edge out the competition by setting yourself apart from the candy salesperson down the block.

Before hitting the street with your box of candy bars, you've sized up the market. From previous wanderings around the neighborhood, you know who will bring out their wallets and who will kindly (or not so kindly) say no thanks. You may even have an idea about what type of candy bars your neighbors prefer so you can choose your candy supply accordingly. You use this information to sell to the folks most likely to buy.

Guess what? You're a marketer. You have used your market knowledge to promote your product to meet sales goals. But how do you apply your candy bar sales experience to promoting your business?

A great place to start is to determine what attributes your company has that provides you with a competitive advantage in the marketplace and then capitalize on those attributes. Competitive advantage means your company's features that differentiate you from your competitors. Three main categories are:

- Cost—You provide similar services to competitors, but at a lower price.
- Quality—Your services may be priced similar to competitors but you offer more services or higher quality services than your competitors.
- Customer service—This means you respond to customer issues and inquiries with greater care than competitors do.

The additional value you create for customers by focusing on one key area differentiates your company from competitors, providing you with competitive advantage. For example, when selling candy bars, your cheery demeanor may give you an advantage over other roving candy salespeople.

One thing to remember—you can't be everything to everyone. Trying to lead in all differentiating categories can drain your resources and cause you to lose sight of your true market strengths. Once you have determined what gives you competitive advantage, you need to decide how to make it work for you. One way to do this is to write a marketing plan.

Writing a marketing plan

The marketing plan is similar to your business plan in that it requires analysis of your company, your market, and your industry. It differs in that it also lays out your plan for competing in the market. The marketing plan also helps you and your employees stay on track when "the next best thing in marketing" arises. If the opportunity fits within your plan—go for it. If it veers in a direction that doesn't fit your goals, take a pass. You can build a marketing program without a marketing plan, but without proper analysis and planning you may not see your desired results. The basic elements of a marketing plan follow:

Mission statement

Include your company's mission statement that you developed during your business planning process. As a reminder, the mission statement is a short, written sentence or paragraph that explains your business goals and ideals and broadly describes your product, services, and target market.

Objectives

In this section, explain both your company's objectives in doing business and your marketing objectives. Your company objective could include how you hope to position your company and what you hope to achieve in the marketplace. For example, an objective for a web development company could be: To build the company's position as an industry leader and to remain competitive by providing services using the most current technologies.

Marketing objectives focus on what you want to achieve with your marketing plan. This could include determining if there is a market for your product, finding out which market to serve or deciding if you want to offer a new product or service.

External analysis

External analysis involves researching your market to determine the driving forces that will affect how you market your business to customers. Key areas to study are:

Market size—This includes details on the amount of money spent on products and services similar to yours, demand for your product, and consumer behaviors that drive purchasing.

Market growth—This includes information about the potential for growth in the market. Think about whether it is a niche market with little room for growth, a market that is expanding, or a market that is contracting. Be as detailed as possible.

Competitors—Include a general overview of competitor categories and descriptions of major competitors. Details about how companies compete in the market (such as through word-of-mouth or referrals) are helpful. Also include advertising and promotional expenditures for competitors and marketing tactics they frequently use. This information can often be found in annual reports and on company websites.

Relevant trends—Relevant trends include those that affect the demand for your product and change the marketplace.

Buying patterns—List the groups most likely to purchase your product or service and how they make their purchases. Some questions to ask are: Do the customers buy your product seasonally or is it something they buy year-round? Do they contract for similar services for the long-term or on a per-event basis? How long does is generally take for a customer to complete the buying process? When you understand how your customers make purchases, you can better determine how to serve their needs.

Market segmentation—Identity the different situation factors, operating variables, and demographics that affect the customer breakdown in your market.

Internal analysis

Now it's time to take a look at your company. An analysis of the following areas should be included in your plan:

Product—Provide an overview of the product or service you provide. Be specific. Include information about how your product works, what it looks like, what your service entails, and any other relevant product information.

Place—Place is an overview of where you sell your product or service. Include any specific cities or geographic regions you serve and restrictions that limit the locations you serve.

Promotion—Include how you currently promote your business.

Pricing—Determine how you will price your product. Review price trends among your competitors. For example, when I first started consulting, I provided a quote to a customer for web design. The cost I quoted was $500, not knowing the company already had a quote for $10,000. I wasn't offering the bells and whistles that the other company included in their quote, but I could have come in around $3,000. It a good idea to survey competitors to see what the going rate for your service is to avoid pricing too high or too low. Also consider your costs. Since your ultimate goal is to make a profit, choose a selling price that covers expenses while leaving room for profit.

Company factors—List items unique to your company's operations that will affect your marketing decisions. This can include the risk level you are willing to take to remain competitive. It can also include your priorities for growing your business. For example, if you offer a web consulting service and your competitive advantage is quality, your priority may be to put financial resources towards maintaining your technology systems. You may also hire staff and contractors that are highly trained in the technologies your company uses.

Market factors—Market factors include such things as your customer base, the current market climate, how sales growth is measured, and geographic factors.

SWOT Analysis

The next section of your marketing plan is the internal versus external analysis, or SWOT analysis. This is similar to the SWOT analysis you performed when creating your business plan, however your lists should include items general to the marketplace, not specific to your company. To start writing this section, assess your company's strengths and weaknesses as they relate to the marketplace. Also, make a list of opportunities and threats that exist in the marketplace that will affect your company.

For example, include government regulations that may have a positive impact on the market. Other areas to include are trends, market conditions, economic conditions, changing rules and standards, and changes in market demand for your product. Use the information you included in the previous sections to perform the analysis.

Choosing marketing alternatives

The final step in your marketing plan is to develop a set of marketing alternatives that support the conclusions you have drawn from your research into the market and your company review. The alternatives should be concise and should focus on what you will do, not how you will do it. Marketing planning is more than creating a brochure or website. Those are marketing tools to support your chosen alternative. The alternatives you identify should revolve around pricing, place, product, and promotion.

For example, if the marketing plan is for a web design company that hopes to expand its services the alternatives could be:

- Alternative 1: Add web development capabilities to serve current client base better.

- Alternative 2: Partner with a web development provider that has programming capabilities.
- Alternative 3: Expand services to include copywriting for websites.

Your final step is to choose an alternative and describe your plan for making the alternative successful. This is where you include information about the marketing tools, also known as the marketing mix, you will incorporate.

The marketing mix

A successful marketing campaign begins with knowing your audience's habits. You should gather two types of information: general industry information and detailed customer information. Use your general industry knowledge to assess your customer's communication preferences. Research the following:

- Where your customers get their information.
- What type of advertising they are likely to respond to.
- When the ideal time to communicate with them is.

Knowing this information will increase your chances that your marketing message will fall on receptive ears. For example, if your business sells gardening supplies you may be aware of industry magazines that your customers read. You also know that your customers plan their purchases prior to the growing season. Therefore, you may want to place an ad introducing your new product line in a popular gardening journal in February or March, prior to the growing season.

Also, gather detailed information about your customers. Some items to include in your customer profiles are:

- Customer's first and last name
- The customer's business name
- The customer's address
- What products they have purchased
- How often they purchase your products
- When they make their purchasing decisions
- The contact information for company purchasing agents

Your profile can be as detailed as you think necessary. Consider your level of comfort with the information you are collecting. Some companies find out information including customers' birthdays, organizations they belong to, even how many children they have. Others just stick to the basics.

Gathering customer information doesn't have to be an expensive proposition. Online and paper-based surveys, customer profile information recorded at the time of a first sale, and face-to-face or phone conversations are simple ways to find out about your customers. Any information you gather about customers can be stored in your customer database. Always make it clear to your customers that the information you are gathering will be kept private and will not be sold or shared with other companies. Strong customer relationships are based on trust.

With the information you have gathered you can now target your marketing to your customers. Targeted marketing means knowing enough about your customers and prospects that you can create marketing campaigns that appeal to their specific tastes. Your marketing message is also placed in locations where your audience is most likely to see it. This differs from mass marketing where your marketing message is placed in the broad marketplace for anyone to see.

There are many marketing avenues you can take, but for small businesses the most accessible are networking, print marketing and web marketing.

Networking

One way to target your market is through networking. Networking is an ongoing process of identifying people that can have a positive impact on your business. Building a successful network takes time, but it is well worth the investment for small businesses.

If you are an industry insider, having worked as an employee of a company that produces your product or service, you have a head start. You may already have a good understanding of the landscape in which you will be operating. You may even have developed relationships that you can capitalize on when you go out on your own.

If you haven't been employed in the industry you will operate in, you likely have an idea of how the industry functions and who the key players are. In either case, it is valuable to stay connected. Attend industry conferences and trade shows, join trade groups, and talk with others about your business.

By positioning yourself at events and locations frequented by industry insiders you will not only learn what business tools and processes are common in the industry, you also will gain valuable contacts. Trade business cards with other professionals in the field; they may be future customers or partners.

Networking isn't reserved for face-to-face venues. With today's technology, networks are popping up throughout the web sphere. Online social networking sites provide great potential for building your network. Search for sites geared to professionals and businesses. These are most likely to have members open to making business connections. Some sites have topical groups you can join. You'll be able to learn about your industry and business in general from others with similar interests.

To make the most of your time online, reserve a designated amount of time each week to join in social networking discussions. Keep your conversations on-point and look for individuals with experience that can benefit your business.

Making connections is just the start. Fostering ongoing relationships with potential business associates can be as simple as having a friendly conversation at a trade show or returning a vendor's phone call. And remember, the people in your network also have a network.

Here is a simple example. Just after launching his business, a hopeful plant seller held a garage sale and displayed some of his plants. A neighbor came to the garage sale, saw the plants and asked a few gardening questions. She didn't buy anything but a few weeks later her mother contacted the budding businessman to order plants for a large landscaping project. Networking works.

And networking is affordable. If your business does not have a large budget for advertising, networking provides a low-cost option for raising your profile in the marketplace. Many organized networking opportunities through business associations, universities and networking clubs are free or have small fees. Online social networking sites are generally free. Talking with a potential customer, vendor or business associate costs nothing but a few minutes of your time. Your network will grow as your business grows.

But beware. As a business owner, it's a struggle knowing when to sell your wares and when to take off your business hat and be a civilian. It's not an easy call. Your network is often the lifeline of your business. Making connections means making sales. But some places require caution. Weddings (I've been accosted by voracious sales folks at one or two), graduations, birthday parties, baby showers, even sporting events are times for showing restraint.

If someone asks about your business—go ahead and share the details but avoid the hard sell. In locations such as grocery stores, coffee shops, community festivals, your local park, and other areas where casual conversations happen, size up the audience and the opportunity. If the situation looks favorable for promoting your business—go for it. Be friendly, be honest, and make the connection.

Print marketing

Print marketing includes communications vehicles like brochures, postcards, flyers, inserts, and advertisements. Marketing pieces such as newsletters, annual reports, sales letters and even advertisements included with invoices also fit into this category.

When considering what type of print marketing materials to develop, use the results of your customer and industry research to determine which type of vehicle is most appealing to your customers. If you plan to attend seminars and/or trade shows, brochures, postcards, and flyers may be good options as promotional pieces. Or, if your customers read a specific trade journal, placing an ad in that journal could generate leads. Gear your marketing to your audience's preferences to get the greatest return on your investment.

When planning your marketing pieces, be alert to timelines. Creating a marketing calendar is a good way to plan around important dates. Record all seminars and trade shows you will attend, all advertising deadlines for trade and consumer publications you will advertise in and any dates of importance to your marketing program. These dates should include any days of importance to your customers such as holidays, product launch dates, and peak purchasing times. Then estimate how long it will take you to produce your marketing pieces and add your development deadlines to the calendar.

Some marketing pieces can take several weeks to produce because you will need to write content, take photos, complete design work, and print the pieces. Magazine or newspaper advertisements could require long lead times due to print scheduling requirements. Sales letters could be produced quickly and should be scheduled for a less development time.

Sometimes marketing opportunities come up with little notice. If a marketing opportunity becomes available, make sure to add it to the calendar and shuffle other projects as needed. Quick-to-produce pieces such as postcards and flyers work well for tight deadlines.

To get the most punch out of your marketing pieces, choose a design that is attractive and copy that is snappy and states your message clearly. If you or your staff have design and copywriting skills, you can produce your marketing materials in-house. If not, freelance designers or design agencies can provide the design expertise.

Your ultimate goal is to encourage potential customers to act on the prompts in your marketing pieces. For example, your marketing piece may say, "Save 20%, Buy now, Call Us or Check Us Out Online." Get to your point quickly, with as few words as possible, consistently and in an interesting way. Sloppy design and poor copyrighting can make your company look amateurish. Spend the time and money to produce quality marketing pieces.

You don't have to break the bank to create well-designed pieces, but plan to invest anywhere from $200 to a few thousand dollars or more depending on the quantity of materials you need. You can often save money by printing your pieces with an online print provider or local print shop and buying in bulk.

After you have printed your marketing pieces, use them. I worked with a client who stockpiled marketing pieces to save them for the big clients. The problem with that strategy was that the big clients could be counted on one hand. He had some beautiful marketing pieces collecting dust in his garage.

Marketing only works if someone sees it. So be brave and mail those sales letters, post your flyers, and hand out your brochures.

Digital marketing

Digital marketing means using websites, email, social media, and other digital channels to expand your company's reach.

Before making purchasing decisions, consumers search the Internet for product information, cost comparisons, and reviews. As a small company, having a digital presence can mean the difference between gaining a new customer or sending them to the competition.

An online presence could mean a social media business profile, an individual website, a blog, or a mix of several digital options. It's important to consider if your team can keep multiple channels current and active.

Otherwise, it can be helpful to focus on whichever channel reaches your audience. Some small businesses start with a social media profile on key platforms to build up an audience and then expand into a business website. They might add a blog or online newsletter to the mix as business and teams grow. When choosing which digital channels to use, consider how media and technically savvy your audience is, where they are likely to search for information, and the time commitment needed to maintain each channel.

Website marketing

When planning a website, be aware that sites that merely mirror your company brochure don't cut it. Customers expect to see pricing, in-depth product details, news about your company, even videos showing how your products work.

To choose content for your site, start with a list of what you want your customers to know and add anything your customers may have asked about during past conversations. Don't forget company and contact information.

To build a website, work with a professional web designer and/or developer. While you can build a site using consumer-friendly web design software and tools, a professional will build your site based on web standards and good design practices.

A knowledgeable web person can also help you find a company to host your site and offer recommendations about how to maintain your site. Many web professionals can also optimize your site so it will have a better showing in search engine results lists.

Social networking

Traditional marketing relies on one-way communication, meaning marketing messages are pushed out to the audience with no direct audience response. Social networking via social media makes two-way communication between a business and customer possible.

Social media works by providing open spaces for people to communicate about anything and everything with a network of friends, family, and anyone allowed access to their social networking pages. Pithy comments, jokes, memes, and reviews can spread quickly among users for the channel. The prospect of open communication with customers is exciting and the potential for quick word-of-mouth messaging is a marketer's greatest dream come true.

A business with a page on a social networking site has a great resource for communicating upcoming events and sales and for seeking general publicity about their product. Customer feedback can be instructive in planning product launches and traditional marketing campaigns. And best of all, social networking is often free, although customer targeting and additional marketing options can be costly.

There are caveats to social networking. Because communications are uncensored (within the restrictions placed on users by the site owners) businesses don't have control of the messaging. If a company stumbles with a product offering, customer service approach, or marketing campaign, word can spread quickly through social networking sites. One unhappy customer can rapidly notify thousands of their displeasure. This is not a new threat. Companies have always been aware of the power of word-of-mouth communication. But social networking increases that power tenfold.

The best protection against negative feedback is to provide top quality service, products that live up to company promises, and honest communication when faced with criticism.

Blogs

Blogs are another form of social networking that operate a bit more like traditional marketing tools such as newsletters or press releases. Blog tools provide a framework for posting quick news-like items that the public can comment on. Blogs also provide a business with building a more personal connection with consumers through storytelling and idea sharing.

Blogs differ from social networking sites in that bloggers choose specific topics on which to report, such as world events, entertainment activities, industry issues, or personal stories that support the company's vision and identity. Bloggers play a reporting role and publish their writings for public comment if they choose.

Company blogs work best when providing informative, timely information to customers. Upcoming events are great. Writing about the results of those events and how they impact customers is even better. Offering instruction on how to use a new product or explaining a changed feature is also a good use of blogs. If you know your industry well, it will be easier to choose blog topics likely to stir customers' interests.

If you decide to include blogging into your marketing mix, be aware that blogging requires time, imagination, and exceptional writing skills. Success can be hard to measure and some industries may see better results than others.

Paid web advertising

Paid web advertising services offered through popular search engines and social media sites provide another opportunity to boost awareness of your company if you serve web savvy customers. Paid web advertising offers several advantages:

- You can manage the position of your website's link on the search results page by offering a competitive bid on chosen search terms.
- You can target advertising to the appropriate audience by choosing search terms your customers use frequently.
- You can measure the value of paid advertising by reviewing statistical reports provided by the advertising service providers.

As an example of how paid web advertising can boost awareness of a website, I viewed search statistics for a client's key product, a specialized type of medical software. The search statistics indicated that web surfers performed 1,657 searches on the key phrase. However, when I ran a search on the same key phrase the client's website didn't show up, but competitors' sites did—many as paid advertisers. Paid advertising can be expensive to achieve measurable results so it's important to have a clear understanding of your business goals and do research into how best to achieve them. Hiring a professional with experience in this area is a good option.

E-newsletters

E-newsletters are a handy marketing tool because they are sent directly to subscribers. Not only are these people interested in what your company has to say, if they find your newsletter valuable, they may forward it to people in their network of friends and acquaintances. This "word of mouth" marketing is a good option for expanding your customer base. When people hear about your company from people they trust, they are more likely to trust your company, try your products, and recommend you to others.

In addition to being an effective marketing tool, e-newsletters offer several practical advantages:

- They are cost-effective because they don't require printing like traditional newsletters.
- E-newsletters can be distributed quickly because e-mail is instantaneous. This works in your favor when you have timely news to share.
- Newsletter subscribers may be open to receiving additional promotional materials from you. Make the option available when you sign up subscribers. (This is called permission marketing).
- E-newsletters can include subscribe/unsubscribe options which make database maintenance simple.
- Third-party e-newsletter management companies make newsletter design and distribution simple. You can find companies that provide e-newsletter

services by running an Internet search using the keyword "e-newsletters."

Because e-newsletters are a powerful communication medium, use them wisely. Your newsletters should be more than a cleverly disguised sales pitch. Include news that benefits your customers. Industry news, company happenings, product information, new product launches, upcoming events, and sales make good stories.

Also, treat your subscribers well. Only send to people that have subscribed to your newsletter. Unwanted e-mails are called spam and are considered bad etiquette. Store subscriber names in a database or use a third-party e-newsletter site to track your mailings. If someone wants to unsubscribe, honor his or her wishes and remove them from your list immediately.

Finally, accept suggestions. Your ultimate goal is to woo customers to your company. Using your e-newsletter to spur two-way communication is an excellent way to build rapport with your customers. Include a link or contact information in your newsletter where subscribers can leave comments. Address those comments when appropriate by incorporating them into your newsletters or business. Sometimes customers are the best marketers your company has.

Influencers

Influencers, people who draw attention to a business often through online formats, can be a powerful tool for small businesses looking to expand their customer base. Influencers leverage their online presence and engaged followers to build trust for a brand and raise its profile.

Unlike traditional advertising, influencer marketing feels more personal and authentic and followers may view influencers as peers rather than salespeople. When an influencer shares a product or service, it can spark curiosity and drive immediate interest, especially if the content is creative, relatable, or includes a personal testimonial.

For small businesses with limited marketing budgets, partnering with micro-influencers—those with smaller but highly dedicated audiences—can be especially effective and cost-efficient. These influencers often have stronger engagement rates and can target niche markets that align closely with the business's ideal customer.

Additionally, influencer content can be repurposed across the business's own social media channels, boosting credibility and reach. Collaborations can take many forms, from product reviews and giveaways to behind-the-scenes content or tutorials.

Ultimately, influencers help small businesses build brand awareness, generate word-of-mouth buzz, and convert followers into loyal customers. With the right partnerships, even a single post can lead to a noticeable uptick in traffic, inquiries, and sales.

Putting the customer first

A happy customer is often a return customer and courting return customers is easier on the bottom line then expending resources always searching for new customers. But small blunders can send even the most loyal customers to the competition without even a wave goodbye.

A little upfront time spent improving your customer service approach will save the headache of trying to repair damaged customer relationships.

Respond to emails and phone calls

In today's fast-paced environment, customers expect timely communication. Quick responses show that a company values its customers' time and concerns, reinforcing a sense of reliability and professionalism. Whether the inquiry involves a product issue, billing question, or general feedback, addressing it swiftly can prevent small problems from escalating and demonstrate a commitment to service excellence.

For potential customers, a fast reply can be the deciding factor between choosing your business or a competitor. For existing clients, it strengthens loyalty and encourages repeat business.

Efficient communication helps streamline operations, reduce backlog, and improve team productivity. It also provides valuable insights into customer needs and expectations, which can inform future improvements. In industries where timing is critical—such as hospitality, retail, or tech support—delayed responses can directly impact revenue and customer retention.

Ultimately, responsiveness is more than just good manners; it's a strategic advantage that fosters positive relationships, drives growth, and sets a company apart in a competitive market.

Honor appointments

There is nothing quite as frustrating for a customer than scheduling an appointment with a business or service provider only to be kept waiting. Or worse yet, to be stood up.

Remember, customers may need to take time off work or juggle other appointments to meet with you. If you are detained, plan to be no more than five minutes late and call to let the customer know you are on your way. Reschedule your appointment when necessary but do so with 24-hour notice so the disruption to the customer's schedule is minimized. Keep appointment rescheduling to a minimum and make sure the client has a consistent contact when scheduling appointments.

Also, consider providing a reasonable window of time to let the customer know when you will arrive for the appointment. The shorter the window, the better so the customer can plan their day to reduce the impact of time away from work or other activities.

Respond to information requests

When someone requests information about your company via email, a website form, over the phone or through some other means, he or she expects a response.

When a company fails to respond, whether due to poor organization, incorrect contacts or a busy schedule, customers are left feeling abandoned.

Have a policy in place for responding to information requests. For example, make it clear to customers that you will respond to their questions and requests within a pre-determined timeframe. Make sure all your employees are aware of the policy and stick to it. Your customers will thank you!

Keep promises

If you promise to complete a job by a specific date, do so. If you offer a money-back guarantee, honor it. If you advertise a 24-hour response time, you had better make sure you contact your customer within 24-hours.

If you cannot keep your promises, it is better not to make them or at least be realistic about what your company's capabilities are. When you make a promise to customers, they will hold you to it.

Say hello

When a customer walks into your business, show them they matter. Welcoming each customer as they enter your business is a simple yet powerful way to create a positive first impression and foster a positive environment. It signals attentiveness, respect, and appreciation, all qualities that build trust and encourage repeat visits.

When customers feel seen and valued from the moment they walk in, they're more likely to engage, stay longer, and make purchases. Ignoring a customer, even unintentionally, can lead to feelings of neglect or frustration, which may drive them elsewhere.

Acknowledgment doesn't require elaborate gestures; small actions go a long way. A warm smile, eye contact, and a friendly greeting like "Welcome in!" or "Let me know if you need anything" can instantly set the tone. If staff are busy, a quick nod or "I'll be right with you" reassures the customer that they're not being overlooked.

For returning customers, using their name or recalling past interactions adds a personal touch that strengthens loyalty. In high-traffic settings, signage or a host at the entrance can help manage flow while still making guests feel acknowledged.

Consistent and thoughtful greetings create a customer-centric atmosphere that reflects professionalism and care, qualities that distinguish great businesses from average ones. A simple acknowledgment goes a long way towards building good will. And good will is the basis of strong business relationships that stand the test of time.

Example: Painting the town

As a college student, Dave worked for a franchise painting company. Under the franchise structure he ran his paint service like an independent business, meaning he was responsible for his own marketing, hiring and firing of employees, paying for his own insurance and employment taxes, and buying his own supplies. For a percentage of Dave's earnings, the franchise organization provided a list of sales leads and skills training.

Dave made a moderate income, but it wasn't enough to support his employees or provide a reasonable profit. After two years of knocking on doors and competing with other franchisees operating in the same small territory, Dave decided to go it alone. He launched his own paint business in 1995. His mission was to provide a quality professional painting service with exceptional customer service. His goal was to support himself as he continued his education; he was a business major.

For Dave, who wanted to gain experience running his own company, owning a paint company was a good opportunity. Dave's challenge was to promote his new business in a competitive market. He built $200 into his budget for marketing. To determine how to spend his marketing dollars, Dave reviewed his company objectives and wrote up a mini marketing plan.

The plan

As stated earlier, Dave's mission was to provide a quality professional painting service with exceptional customer service.

His main objective was to establish a customer base in his chosen territory by positioning himself as a trusted local painter with roots in the community. He also wanted to limit his business to a level he could manage as a solo painter.

Dave's marketing objective was to increase awareness of his business in his chosen market and to differentiate his company from other house painters serving the market.

External Analysis

Dave lived in a large metro area where construction was booming. In the suburbs, subdivisions sprouted from cornfields and McMansions popped up where ramblers once stood. Even in the densely populated inner city, condos and townhomes were built next to aging houses with peeling paint. Smaller communities at the city's edge grew as people escaped hectic city life for country living. These communities, within an hour's drive of the city consisted of older neighborhoods with new construction littered about.

The combination of new construction and historical homes made the city and its surrounding communities attractive to both independent contractors and painting franchise companies. Since maintenance on a historical house involved challenging manual labor and in some cases an understanding of preservation requirements, experienced contractors, including painters, were in demand.

Labor to staff the franchise companies was plentiful with more than six colleges in the area from which to draw employees. These companies carved out territories across the metro area and assigned painters based on customer demand. Independent contractors served the entire metro area and beyond.

Even though house painting was a crowded field, it wasn't necessarily a lucrative profession. Independent contractors could expect to earn $15 to $20 an hour. A painter working for a franchise could earn $8 to $12 an hour. The hours could be long, with painters sometimes working 12-hour days to finish a project.

From Dave's days as a franchise painter, he knew that homeowners began contacting painters in April and May for summer projects. They hired primarily through referrals and advertisements in the local paper and phone books. Throughout summer, painting jobs were numerous. By fall he could expect three or four jobs. But work would dwindle by mid-October as the temperature dropped and homeowners turned their attention to covering plants and putting plastic on their windows to prepare for the long winter ahead.

Internal Analysis

Dave provided one service—house painting. But house painting was more than dipping a brush in the paint and slopping it on the side of a house. As a part of his service, Dave provided cost estimation, paint recommendations, siding preparation such as scraping old paint, and clean-up. Meeting deadlines was a part of the service, so Dave worked on demand and at unusual hours if needed.

Dave performed his painting services in both the metro area where he lived and in his smaller hometown. In the metro area, he tackled projects near his neighborhood where older homes sat next to more modern apartment buildings.

But Dave focused most of his energy on serving clients in his hometown, a city of 20,000 people. The city was dripping with history and tradition. As such, many of the homes were almost 100 years old and barely updated. This meant painted wood siding instead of vinyl. The going rate for painters in the area was in the $8 to $12 range due to the town's proximity to the city.

While Dave was working for a franchise operation he solicited bids by cold calling, meaning he walked through neighborhoods and knocked on doors. For every 1,000 homes he or his crew visited, they booked three jobs—not a great track record. When Dave launched his business, he decided cold calling was not an option. He was just one person and visiting even 50 houses wasn't realistic. He also didn't have a staff for managing a marketing program on an ongoing basis so he relied on referrals for new business.

SWOT Analysis

Dave had the skills to meet the market demands:

- He had expert training as a painter from his franchisee days and understood the business of painting. He could assess customer needs, provide accurate cost estimates, and complete the job by deadline.
- He had experience managing a business which would put him on par with larger competitors and ahead of those without strong business skills.
- Dave was young and strong. He could work on a job for a full day and into the night if needed.
- He had name recognition and a built-in network of family and friends in his service area. Although he had moved from the area several years before starting his painting business, his roots run deep.

On the downside:

- Dave didn't have a track record as a painter in his local community since he had learned the trade after moving out of the town.
- Dave was also a one-painter operation which meant he wouldn't be able to tackle the more profitable large-scale painting projects.
- Like all house painting businesses, Dave's business was subject to changes in the housing market. Dave's livelihood was threatened by consumers' interests in maintenance-free siding and natural materials such as brick and stone.
- Dave faced competition from other independent contractors and larger paint companies.

But opportunities were plentiful. Construction was booming, providing ample work for painters. For Dave the construction boom provided an opportunity to fill a niche, because many painters doubled as construction contractors. When they were pulled onto building sites, Dave could fill the gap and serve homeowners with older homes needing fresh paint. Because he focused on existing buildings rather than new construction he also was less affected by the fits and starts of the housing market.

The housing boom had another side-effect that benefited Dave's company. With the boom came high home prices. People priced out of the market were fueling the demand for remodeling contractors. As owners of older houses built new living spaces, they needed painters to put the finishing touches on their happy homes. For people on tight budgets, painting was a low-cost alternative to major renovations.

After getting a good feel for the market and assessing his capabilities to operate in that market, Dave developed three marketing alternatives:

- Alternative 1: Serve the painting needs of the metro area and his hometown.
- Alternative 2: Serve homeowners in his hometown exclusively.
- Alternative 3: Expand his business to include new construction.

Dave opted for alternative two because he would be able to target residential properties in areas he was familiar with and use his community connections to secure the work. He wouldn't burn his limited resources trying to compete in the large metro market where competition was high.

Dave set aside $200 in his budget for marketing materials. To reach homeowners in his community he posted flyers on bulletin boards located in local hardware and paint supply stores. He also ran a weekly ad in the classifieds section of the community newspaper. Finally, he engaged the help of his family and friends to generate leads for his business. Through referrals and calls received from people responding to his ads,

Dave's business earned $10,000 during its first three months in business.

Chapter 9:
Master of all trades...not

As the owner of a small business, you are a salesperson, operations manager, marketer, service provider, bookkeeper...and somewhere in there you're still a person with a life. When life and leisure become a vague memory, and sleep is something you do between phone calls and paperwork, it's time for HELP.

Hiring help is a big step for any organization, but especially for a small business. You need to set up a payment system, learn a new set of tax rules, and make sure you file the right legal documents. You also need to find talented people who share your vision to build your business alongside you.

Hiring employees, whether on staff or in consulting roles, is a big step for any business. It's a sign that your business is growing. In the pit of your stomach, you feel excited at the prospect of finding a cohort to work alongside you...or is it dread?

With small businesses, choosing the right person is of the utmost importance because your resources are limited. It takes time and money to find prospective candidates and then to hire and train an employee. Your focus on other aspects of your business is waylaid while you search for that perfect individual to round out your staff.

Before jumping into hiring, it's important to determine your staffing needs and make sure they support your plan for business growth.

Filling a skills gap

If you can crunch numbers, write hard-hitting ad copy, and negotiate a contract, all while designing your company's products and performing your key services—bravo! If you can't, that's okay. No one is an expert at everything. Even the most successful business owners have gaps in their knowledge. When these knowledge gaps hinder your company's success it's time to bring in help.

Focus on your expertise and find others who have the skills to fill the gaps in your knowledge. To determine where you have a skills gap in your business, list tasks that are critical to your success but fall outside your area of expertise. For example, you may excel at product development but struggle with financial management, digital marketing, or legal compliance. These areas are where you would focus your hiring efforts.

It's common for small companies to hire accountants, lawyers, technology consultants, projects managers, and customer service personnel on a contract, part-time, or full-time basis.

As your business grows, continue to review your operations to identify areas where specialized skills are needed so you can stay competitive in the marketplace.

Pay considerations

Determining employee pay involves a balance between what your business can afford and market value for an employee's skillset and experience. To find the right pay range for a job position takes research and careful planning.

When creating a position, make a list of the tasks the employee will perform. Create another list of the skills that you are looking for in an employee. For example, if you are looking for an accountant to keep your books, one requirement may be that the individual is a Certified Public Accountant (CPA). A CPA will command a higher pay rate than someone with a general accounting education. However, if you are looking for an individual to perform general office work such as stuffing envelopes and filing, an entry level person may be a good fit.

Use the position descriptions you have developed to determine market pay rates for similar positions. The Internet is a useful source for pay scale information. Visit employment websites to find similar job descriptions to your own. Many states now require salary information to be posted in employment listings. The Bureau of Labor Statistics also has salary data free to the public. Your research will help you find a level where you can realistically set the pay scale to attract the right employee.

Other factors to consider are:
- Market competition for the particular position you are hiring for
- Type of position—full-time, part-time, or contract hours
- Type of benefits you will provide
- Location of the position
- Length of contract for a contract position
- Experience level— Entry level versus experienced

Keep in mind that when setting pay rates for a position, it's important that compensation is both equitable and free from bias. Equitable pay means offering salaries that are fair and consistent for similar roles, regardless of an employee's gender, race, age, or other personal characteristics. Decisions based on objective criteria such as market rates, required skills, experience, and job responsibilities helped avoid bias in hiring and pay.

Prioritizing pay transparency and fairness helps businesses comply with legal requirements and build a culture of trust.

Managing the work of others

Success or failure in hiring often hinges on compatibility between manager and employee. Know your management style before hiring. If you have management experience, you may be aware of your leadership style and what type of employees fit well in your organization.

If you never managed people, it's a good time to think about how you work with others. Think about how you performed your work when you were an employee:

- Did you prefer to work alone or with a team?
- Did you enjoy the little details or were you more interested in the "big picture?"
- Are you relaxed in your working relationships with others or do you prefer others to stay on task?
- Do you hide from conflict or thrive on problem solving?

Unless you want to hire sparring partners rather than employees, be realistic about your expectations for your employees and yourself. Here are some examples of commonly accepted management profiles to consider when hiring employees:

- *You enjoy directing the work of others or mentoring staff members.* Early career employees may work well. Just avoid becoming a micro manager. Even beginners need decision-making freedom to grow their talents.

- *You like to focus on "big picture" aspects of your business and have your employees handle the details.* Hiring experienced workers who can manage most aspects of their own work may be a good fit. Just make sure to check in with your employees so you are in the loop on the work status.
- *You are more comfortable managing projects than people.* Experienced, self-directed workers and independent contractors may be a nice fit. However, be aware that managing people issues comes with owning a business.

Ease the transition into management

You've heard the phrase, people don't quit jobs, they quit managers. But why are those managers not well-suited for management? They were likely good employees who were promoted due to their talent or success at achieving company goals, but skill doesn't always translate into management strengths. Some new managers or people pursuing management roles seek additional training to learn the skills needed to manage well, but many don't. Instead, they move up the ranks picking up habits from their peers and leaders. Some habits are useful, some are not.

If you truly want to excel at people management, keep the following tips in mind as you grown into your role.

It's not about you. Once you become a manager, you're not the star of the show like you were as an individual contributor. You might have won awards, been touted for your sales numbers, and received pats on the back when you walked down the halls. None of that matters now. The spotlight is on your team and your job is to help them shine. Your team members each have a role to play and your job is to make sure they can play that role to the best of their abilities. Sometimes that means providing direction then getting out of the way so your team can do what they do best.

Your team is made up of individuals, not numbers. Each team member is unique. You might have introverts, extroverts, people of different cultural backgrounds, people at different skill levels. No two team members are alike. These differences are what make your team great.

You can create a high-performing team by personalizing your management style to meet the individual needs of your team members. This means communicating in multiple ways or customizing communications to meet team members' preferences. Email might work well for one team member, while another might prefer face-to-face. Some team members might be more than happy to speak up at group meetings while others prefer to discuss items in private.

Do what works best to create open and positive communication with your team. This doesn't mean your team can't have shared experiences. The team should have consistent standards for behavior, quality, goals and other operational considerations. Just be flexible in how you interact and guide each member of your team so they can be their best selves.

Help people do their jobs. There's nothing worse than a micromanager who looks over a team member's shoulder and constantly criticizes their work. As a manager, your job is to step back and give your team space to do their work. The members of your team are experts at what they do. Your role is to coach employees when they seek input or face struggles with achieving their goals.

If employees work well and don't need your input in their daily work, be proud that you hired well. Compliment and encourage employees to continue to grow and develop, but don't get in their way.

If an employee is falling down in their job, don't step in and do the work for them. Provide steps the employee can take to improve and monitor the situation. Be there to answer questions and check-in from time to time to make sure the employee is comfortable with the direction of the tasks. The end-goal is to see improvement in the employee's skills, not to add the work to your plate.

Listen without judgement. Some managers love to hear themselves talk. It feels authoritative and boss like. Isn't that why we became bosses—to impart knowledge and direct the work of others? The problem is, when you're dominating the conversation, your team isn't being heard.

When you schedule one-on-one time with your team, the team members should do most of the talking. It's the manager's job to actively listen and offer insight where needed. If it's not needed, just listen and learn.

To show you understand what you are hearing, repeat the team member's requests or ideas. Jot down any follow-ups and how you will communicate additional information (email vs in person). Schedule any follow-up meetings that are needed to act on the team member's comments. By really listening to your team, you'll see greater energy and experience successful outcomes.

When all else fails, lead. You are the boss and are an active participant in your teams. Be the leader that guides your team through the daily challenges that they experience. Remove roadblocks, whether they are political, resource-related, or due to competing priorities.

You are charged with making the hard decisions to smooth the way so your team can do what they do best. Don't delegate away your responsibility to lead because you are afraid of making mistakes or standing up for your team in the face of adversity. Be an advocate for what is right and what your team needs to reach its goals. They will thank you by doing their very best work.

Employee availability

Use the job description you have developed to determine the hours needed to complete the tasks. If the employee can be expected to complete the job in less than 30 hours a week, consider hiring part time. If not, you may need someone full-time.

Note that the costs of hiring, such as advertising the position, interviewing and training, can be high for part-time employees if turnover is high. It can be more cost effective to hire a full-time person. However, if you need someone for a limited task, for example making once-a-week updates to your website, the costs of providing pay and benefits to a full-time employee may outweigh the costs of hiring a part-time worker.

Consider hiring a contract employee when there is a specific task or project that requires specialized expertise not available within the current team, or when the workload does not justify a permanent hire.

Contract employees are ideal for short-term assignments, seasonal work, or roles that demand highly technical skills, such as accounting, legal advice, technology consulting, or marketing. This approach allows small businesses to access professional talent without the long-term commitment and costs associated with full-time employment, such as benefits and payroll taxes.

Additionally, hiring contract workers can provide flexibility to scale up or down as business needs change, making it a practical solution for managing limited resources and addressing temporary gaps in skills.

Hiring employees

You have decided to hire help. Now you need to find qualified candidates to do the job. Advertising on employment websites is a good start. Employment agencies can also provide workers for short-term and long-term positions.

Tap former co-workers who may be job hunting as well. Ask friends, family, and associates for referrals. These personal connections may prove to be advantageous in your hunt for employees. Your close acquaintances are unlikely to steer you wrong for fear of being uninvited to the next social gathering. If you are comfortable with social networking sites, you may find candidates there also.

If you are looking for an independent contractor, search your file cabinet, shoe boxes, and briefcase for business cards handed to you by consultants, vendors, and employment agencies that you have run into during your workday. Within your card stash there is bound to be at least a few professionals worth contacting.

Beware of hiring pitfalls when searching for candidates. First, only hire as many employees as you need to complete the available work. It's tempting to think that the more employees you have, the more work you can get done.

However, if you don't have enough work for the employees, productivity can actually decrease. You'll spend valuable time trying to create work for your employees, and that work isn't necessarily core to your business. Too many employees will drain your resources and quickly empty your pockets. Use the detailed job descriptions you wrote as your guide. Only hire to fill the job you have outlined. When the position is full, you are done hiring.

Second, be cautious when hiring friends and relatives. Avoid hiring people just because they are familiar to you or hiring them would be a "favor" to a friend. If the individual has the skills you need, that's wonderful. If you can work alongside them without resorting to childish bickering, great. If you have experience working with the person and know you are compatible, better yet. If not, politely pass them over.

Third, hire for quality—not cost. Candidates may choose to work for less than market value if they hope to gain experience or want to get a foot in the door. Employees who may be entering the job market after an absence or after having been at one job for a long time may also have a skewed understanding of salary levels. But watch out. Inexperience, lack of dependability, checkered job history, past unethical behavior, even criminal activities may be behind the employee's willingness to work for peanuts.

Checking job history and references and running a background check are good ideas when hiring employees, especially those whose compensation expectations are out of synch with the market.

After you have a good list of candidates, start making calls. Screening candidates by phone before face-to-face meetings can help save time during the hiring process. Ask the right questions and you'll be able to refine your list to a few well-qualified individuals. The questions you ask will vary based on the position you are hiring for, but here's some information you may want to gather:

- Examples of the candidate's past job responsibilities or projects that relate to the open position
- A problem the person had to solve and how they found resolution
- An example of candidate's ability to work with others to complete tasks
- Employment history, especially if someone has switched jobs frequently. This can raise red flags as to the candidate's commitment to employment. However, remember that job switching can result from volatile markets and layoffs.

Job candidates who are eager to please will put a positive spin on their desire to work in your organization. It is important that you get the real feel for the candidate's work style and comfort zone. Explain your organization and your management style in general terms. Ask the candidate if they are comfortable working under those conditions.

Now that you've selected an employee, put your offer of employment in writing. For staff employees, a letter outlining the terms of the position is appropriate. Some items to include in the offer follow:

- Position title
- A description of the job responsibilities
- Whether the position is full-time or part-time
- The hours and whether there is flexibility
- The location of the job (if it is a work-from-home job make sure to specify that information)
- Start date and end date if applicable
- Pay rate or salary
- If employment is at will, meaning the employee can leave at any time and the employer can end the employee's employment at any time.
- Any requirements before starting the position such as filling out tax forms or other paperwork

You may decide to hire an independent contractor instead of a staff employee if you need someone to complete a specific task within a limited time frame.

In general, an independent contractor is a person who manages his or her own work and work hours, pays his or her own taxes, doesn't receive benefits from the hiring organization, and works for multiple clients at the same time.

Some independent contractors work off site and maintain their own equipment. Others may work in your office, but do not have a permanent office space. Make sure you aren't treating contractors like employees because this can lead to legal and tax issues. The IRS, state tax agencies, and the U.S. Department of Labor can provide guidelines about working with independent contractors.

For independent contractors, develop a contract that lays out the specific tasks the employee will perform, the timelines for completing the work, and the pay rate. Contract employees or the agencies that represent them may have standard contracts prepared. Always review the contracts to make sure the tasks the employee will perform are outlined and the terms of the agreement are acceptable. If you are hiring a contract employee that doesn't produce a contract, draft your own.

Examples of these types of contracts can be found on the Internet. If the position's responsibilities or terms of employment are complex, consider hiring an attorney to draft the contract. Make sure you and the employee sign the contract and both have copies for your files. Having a detailed contract will help alleviate any questions about the position that may crop up.

You may also want to have contractors and employees sign a non-disclosure agreement. By signing this document, the contractor or employee agrees not to share your company's proprietary information with others. This is especially important if you are in a competitive industry that relies on insider knowledge, such as financial services and technology.

Paperwork

With employees comes paperwork. As an employer you have tax-related responsibilities including withholding social security and Medicare taxes from employee wages and paying your share of these taxes. You are also required to pay the federal unemployment tax. This tax supports the unemployment benefits employees can tap into after losing a job. Visit the IRS website or talk to a tax professional to learn more about how to calculate employment taxes.

Here is a list of some of the forms you may need:
- Form I-9, Employment Eligibility Verification. The employee fills out this form to verify he or she can legally work in the United States.
- Form W-2. Use this form to gather the employee's name and social security number.
- Form W-4, Employee's Withholding Allowance Certificate. Employees complete this form to verify

how much income tax to withhold from each paycheck.

- Form 941, Employer's Quarterly Federal Tax Return. Use this form to report federal income, Social Security, and Medicare taxes.
- Form 1099-MISC. Use this form to report payments made to an independent contractor.

If you have employees, your state may require you to carry workers compensation insurance. This insurance protects you from lawsuits related to employee injuries that occur on the job. Injured employees receive payments to help with medical bills and cover expenses while the employee is away from work. Workers compensation insurance is purchased separately from your other insurance policies. Check with your state to determine workers compensation requirements.

You're hired! onboarding your new employee

You've extended an offer and your candidate has accepted. The ink is dry and the paperwork is filed. Your eager employee is standing at your desk with high aspirations. Now what?

On your employee's or consultant's first day with your company provide as much company background information as you think is necessary for the employee to perform his or her responsibilities. Include information about the market you do business in and important strategies and goals the employee needs to know. You may have introduced this information at a high level to your employee during the interview process. Now get to the nuts and bolts.

- Explain your role with the company and make sure the employee understands his or her role. Misunderstandings about roles and responsibilities can lead to poor outcomes with the working relationship.
- Outline any policies and ways of doing business that you feel are important to the employee's success with your company.
- Address your expectations for employee behavior including how clients/customers are managed, when the employee is expected to be in the office, and restrictions on the use of office equipment.
- If the employee will be working off site, explain reporting requirements. For example, if you expect the employee to call in or email every day, make that clear. If a weekly face-to-face meeting is enough, determine how that will occur.
- Answer any questions that the employee may have about the business. These may be as complex as how do we set ourselves apart from our biggest competitor or as simple as, "Where's the bathroom?"

- Consider having an open-door policy. This means the employee can come to you to ask a question or discuss an issue at any time you are available without scheduling a special meeting. The goal of the open-door policy is to create an atmosphere of openness and trust.
- Provide any training on software, processes, or other day-to-day operational procedures that company requires employees to use.

Finally, take the new employee to lunch. A double cheeseburger does wonders to ease first day jitters.

Example: You're fired!

When businesses hire, they hope it's for keeps. A long-lasting relationship with employees is as beneficial to the company as it is to the employee. No business owner wants to see company knowledge walk out the door when an employee leaves and training replacement employees is an expensive time drain. But sometimes employee/employer relationships fail and employees are shown the exit door.

Firing an employee is hard. It happens due to poor work performance, personality conflicts, and inappropriate employee behavior. For all businesses, but especially small businesses without vast human resources departments and layers of policies and procedures, the fallout from an employee firing can be hazardous if the case isn't handled properly.

A small-business owner who ran a graphic design studio found out the hard way that firing employees isn't a cakewalk. The studio owner hired a communications consultant to help draft employee manuals, marketing materials, and press releases. The writer worked at home and came to the office once a week for staff meetings. She received assignments via e-mail and phone and submitted her work through e-mail. She was paid biweekly by check sent through the mail.

The relationship started wonderfully. The consultant completed her assignments by deadline and with quality work. After several weeks of working with the consultant, the owner remained impressed and printed business cards to cement her relationship with the company. Then he invited her to a company-sponsored lunch.

At the end of the consultant's fourth week, he invited her and a few other contractors to lunch as a thank you for their work. The restaurant was nothing fancy, just a local hamburger joint where good conversation was plentiful. The group sat around the table chatting and relaxing. The mood was jovial. The discussions were light. But then the conversation turned to business. The owner mentioned his goals for the year.

The communications consultant, who was fresh out of college and was bursting with opinions, decided to provide her input. She was brash and bold, not yet having learned the art of diplomacy. The studio owner had not opened the floor to discussion and was not interested in the consultant's opinion. A toe-to-toe battle of egos ensued. The other contractors sat quietly hiding behind their napkins and water glasses as the owner and communications consultant waged a war of words. After ten minutes the business owner was bruised but not beaten. He had the ultimate weapon and he used it.

"This has been an eye-opening lunch. Let's call it a day." He waved the nervous contractors toward the door. They were more than eager to oblige. He turned to the communications consultant as she gathered up her coat and purse and quietly said, "I don't think our arrangement is going to work out so let's call it good and go our separate ways."

The communications consultant was stunned. She didn't realize her input offended the owner. She had enjoyed similar intense discussions in college and the outcomes were always positive. What she failed to realize is that conversations over beer with friends are much different than verbal challenges to a business owner who was pouring his time and energy into building his business in the direction he determined most beneficial to the company's bottom line.

The communications contractor drove home and the business owner returned to his office. All was well that ends well, right? Wrong.

The business owner was also young and had little experience handling employee issues. What the consultant expected after losing her job was this: The business owner would send her final paycheck in the mail for work completed, she'd cash it and move on. She wasn't under contract so the final check would have settled the debt.

What happened was this: The business owner didn't send her the final paycheck. The consultant called the company asking when her paycheck would be sent. The business owner had caller ID and didn't pick up when the consultant called. She called several more times without reaching the business owner. She then called a lawyer.

The lawyer recommended that the consultant send a certified letter containing her invoice and requesting her check. She did so, but the business owner didn't send payment. He instead called the consultant and left a message on her phone suggesting that she never worked for the company and therefore wouldn't get paid. After a couple weeks of trading certified letters and nasty voice mail messages with the business owner, the consultant filed a claim in small claims court.

During the court face off, the business owner again tried to say that the consultant never worked for the company, but the business cards, work product in the consultant's possession, and co-worker testimonials proved otherwise. She won her case, the business owner was reprimanded by the judge for his bad behavior, and both parties learned a lesson about the challenges of employee/employer relationships.

Chapter 10:
Managing common risks small business owners face

Running your own business can be exciting and rewarding, but it also comes with challenges. Every small business owner faces risks that could affect sales, operations, or even long-term survival. The key is to understand these risks early and make smart plans to reduce them.

Financial risks

Money problems are one of the biggest reasons small businesses fail. Financial risk includes things like not having enough startup funds, unexpected expenses, or customers who don't pay on time. You might also face cash flow issues if your income doesn't match your monthly costs.

For example, you open a small coffee shop and business is good, but your espresso machine breaks down suddenly. You didn't plan for such a large repair bill, and now you're short on cash to buy supplies. You may find yourself underwater quickly without a plan.

Carefully managing your finances is essential to protecting your business from unexpected setbacks and long-term instability. Financial risks, such as cash shortages, seasonal slumps, or rising costs, can quickly derail operations if not addressed proactively.

One of the most effective strategies is creating a detailed budget that accounts for all expenses, including rent, utilities, marketing, and equipment. This helps you plan ahead and avoid overspending.

Building an emergency fund is also important; saving at least three months' worth of operating costs provides a cushion during slow periods or unforeseen events. Monitoring your cash flow with accounting software allows you to track income and expenses in real time, making it easier to spot trends and adjust accordingly.

Finally, diversifying your income by offering new products or services can reduce dependence on a single revenue stream and increase financial resilience. Together, these practices create a strong foundation for sustainable growth and long-term success.

Market risk

The marketplace is constantly evolving, and small businesses must be prepared to adapt. Customer preferences shift, new competitors emerge, and economic changes can influence spending habits. These factors create market risk, where your products or services may lose appeal or your business model may no longer meet demand.

To stay competitive, it's important to conduct regular market research including surveying customers, monitoring trends, and analyzing competitors to understand what's working and what's changing. Flexibility is key; if demand starts to drop, consider adjusting your product mix or pricing strategy to better align with customer needs.

Innovation also helps you stand out. Consider offering custom designs, loyalty rewards, or unique services can attract attention and build customer loyalty.

Finally, keep a close eye on your sales data. A steady decline may be an early warning that your strategy needs a refresh. By staying informed and responsive, you can navigate market shifts and maintain long-term success.

Operational risk

Operational risk stems from internal disruptions that interfere with a business's ability to function smoothly—such as supply chain issues, equipment breakdowns, or staff shortages. These problems can lead to delays, lost revenue, and customer dissatisfaction.

To minimize this risk, proactive planning is essential. One key strategy is to have backup suppliers by building relationships with multiple vendors for critical materials, ensuring continuity if one source fails.

Documenting your systems is equally important; written instructions for daily tasks allow others to step in seamlessly when someone is absent. Cross-training employees to handle multiple roles adds flexibility and resilience, helping the team adapt quickly during unexpected absences or peak periods. Regular maintenance of equipment also plays a vital role—servicing tools and machinery before they break down prevents costly interruptions.

By implementing these measures, your business can maintain consistent operations, respond effectively to challenges, and protect your reputation and bottom line.

Legal and compliance risk

Even small businesses must follow local, state, and federal laws. These include paying taxes correctly, following labor laws, protecting customer data, and keeping safety standards. Breaking rules, even accidentally, can result in penalties or legal trouble.

Make sure to stay current on legal, regulatory, and compliance requirements for your industry and business. Attend workshops or webinars from your local small business association and consult accountants, attorneys and other professionals to make sure you are compliant. Also, keep accurate records in case you are audited of face legal questions or actions.

Contract disputes can also lead to costly legal issues. You might think a handshake or simple email agreement is enough but without a clear written contract, misunderstandings can lead to legal trouble. Always use written contracts that spell out terms clearly including payment, deadlines, responsibilities, and what happens if things go wrong. Work with a lawyer to review all contracts and advise about how best to account for all potential concerns, especially for large deals or partnerships.

Intellectual property (IP) issues

Many small businesses don't realize they can accidentally infringe on someone else's brand, logo, slogan, or even website content. Or they forget to protect their own ideas. This can lead to legal fees, the need to rebrand, or product confusion among customers.

Protecting intellectual property is essential for any business or creative endeavor. Before selecting a name, logo, or slogan, it's important to research existing trademarks to avoid legal conflicts and ensure your brand identity is truly original.

Once you've developed unique assets such as a product design, written content, or branding elements, registering trademarks, copyrights, or patents helps safeguard your work from unauthorized use and establishes legal ownership. This protection not only preserves your competitive edge but also builds credibility with customers and partners.

It's equally important to respect the intellectual property of others. Using online images, music, or written content without proper permission or licensing can lead to costly legal issues and damage your reputation. By taking proactive steps to protect your own creations and honor the rights of others, you foster a culture of integrity and innovation.

Intellectual property protection is not just a legal formality—it's a strategic investment in your brand's future.

Employee misclassification

Misclassifying employees, such as hiring someone as a contractor when they legally qualify as an employee, can result in costly tax penalties, fines, and even lawsuits. Properly classifying workers as either employees or independent contractors is critical for business owners to avoid legal and financial consequences.

Employees are entitled to benefits, protections, and tax withholdings that contractors are not, so it's essential to understand the legal distinctions under both state and federal law. Factors like control over work hours, tools provided, and the nature of the working relationship all play a role in determining classification.

To stay compliant, business owners should maintain accurate payroll records and issue the correct tax forms—W-2 for employees and 1099 for contractors. Taking the time to learn classification rules and apply them correctly not only protects your business from penalties but also builds trust with workers and ensures fair treatment. It's a vital step in responsible business management.

Zoning and permit violations

Starting a small business is exciting, but it's important to understand the legal landscape before launching, especially when operating from home. Even home-based businesses can run into trouble if they overlook local zoning laws and permit requirements.

For example, a home baker who begins selling cupcakes from her kitchen may unknowingly violate residential zoning rules that prohibit commercial food production. As a result, she could face fines and be forced to shut down operations.

To avoid these setbacks, it's crucial to research city and county zoning regulations before launching or expanding a business. Some areas restrict signage, customer traffic, or specific industries in residential zones.

Additionally, securing the correct licenses or permits, such as food handling, retail, or home occupation permits, ensures compliance and protects your business from legal action. Taking these steps early not only prevents costly penalties but also builds a solid foundation for growth.

Whether you're selling online or in person, understanding and respecting local laws helps you operate with confidence and credibility.

Data privacy and customer information

Collecting customer data such as emails, payment details, or browsing history comes with serious legal responsibilities. Businesses must handle this information with care, especially as privacy laws become stricter across states and countries.

For instance, an online store that gathers customer emails without explaining how they're used may face complaints under consumer privacy laws. This can trigger investigations and damage customer trust.

To stay compliant, businesses should post a clear privacy policy on their website that explains data collection, usage, and storage practices. Personal information should be protected with secure systems and deleted when no longer needed.

It's also important to stay informed about state-specific regulations, which may require opt-in consent or data access rights. Respecting customer privacy isn't just about avoiding fines, it's about building loyalty and transparency. When customers feel their information is safe, they're more likely to return and recommend your business.

Discrimination or harassment claims

Discrimination and harassment claims can arise even from unintentional comments or poorly handled workplace conflicts. Small businesses, especially those without formal HR departments, are at greater risk of legal trouble if they don't address these issues proactively.

For example, a manager who makes an offhand remark about an employee's age during a meeting could face a discrimination complaint. To prevent such incidents, businesses should provide basic training on workplace conduct and anti-discrimination laws.
This helps employees understand what's appropriate and how to report concerns.

It's also essential to document all hiring decisions, promotions, and disciplinary actions to show fairness and consistency. When complaints do arise, they should be addressed promptly and professionally to avoid escalation.

Creating a respectful and inclusive work environment not only reduces legal risk but also boosts morale and productivity. Employees who feel safe and valued are more likely to contribute positively to the business.

Partnership or ownership disputes

Starting a business with friends or family can be exciting, but skipping formal agreements often leads to serious disputes. Without clear documentation, disagreements over money, roles, or decision-making can escalate into lawsuits.

For example, two friends who launch a landscaping company without defining ownership percentages may clash when one wants to sell and the other refuses. To prevent this, it's vital to create a partnership or operating agreement early—even for small ventures.

This document should outline ownership shares, responsibilities, decision-making processes, and exit strategies. Putting everything in writing helps clarify expectations and reduces misunderstandings. It also protects the business if one partner leaves or if the company grows and attracts investors.

Formal agreements aren't just for large corporations— they're a smart move for any business. Clear communication and legal structure build trust, prevent conflict, and ensure that everyone is on the same page from day one.

Advertising and marketing claims

False or misleading advertising can land a business in legal trouble, even if the intent wasn't malicious. For example, a skincare company that promotes its lotion as "clinically proven to remove wrinkles" without actual testing may face fines from the Federal Trade Commission (FTC).

To avoid such issues, businesses must be honest and specific in their marketing. Claims like "guaranteed," "proven," or "safe" should only be used if backed by credible evidence. Testimonials, product benefits, and promotional language should be supported by documentation in case of review or complaint.

Misleading customers not only risks legal penalties but also damages trust and brand reputation. Transparency in advertising helps build credibility and long-term loyalty. By focusing on truthful messaging and maintaining records of all claims, businesses can market confidently and ethically. In a competitive landscape, integrity in advertising sets your brand apart and protects it from costly mistakes.

Reputation risk

A business's reputation is one of its most valuable assets and it can be damaged quickly by poor customer interactions or public mistakes.

For example, if a customer leaves a negative review about rude service and the business ignores it, others may believe the same and choose competitors instead.

To protect your reputation, prioritize excellent customer service and treat every guest with respect, especially when resolving complaints. Monitor online feedback regularly, including social media and review platforms, to stay aware of public perception. Responding professionally to criticism by thanking customers for their input and offering solutions shows accountability and care.

Consistency is also key: your brand's tone, values, and messaging should align across all channels. A strong reputation attracts new customers, retains existing ones, and opens doors to partnerships and growth.

In today's digital age, reputation management isn't optional. It's a daily practice that reflects your business's integrity and commitment.

Cybersecurity risk

Cybersecurity is a growing concern for small businesses, which are often targeted by hackers due to limited defenses. Many owners mistakenly believe only large corporations are at risk, but threats like phishing scams, ransomware, and data breaches affect businesses of all sizes.

To reduce risk, use strong, unique passwords and change them regularly. Install and update antivirus software to block malicious attacks. Back up important data to secure cloud storage to prevent loss during a breach. Train employees to recognize suspicious emails or links, and limit system access to only those who need it.

Cybersecurity isn't just a technical issue—it's a business priority. Protecting customer information and internal data helps maintain credibility, avoid legal consequences, and ensure long-term success.

Chapter 11:
Thinking about the future

I cringe every time I hear somebody say, "I do my work this way because that's how it's always been done." Change is hard. It requires stepping outside the comfort zone and trying something new. But change is necessary to move a business forward. When the world pivots, businesses needed to work differently to survive.

So how do companies stay ahead of the curve? They innovate. New ways of working can improve efficiency, bring in more customers by creating more opportunities, and often reduce costs.

Best ways to encourage innovation

The number one source for innovative ideas is the employees who work with processes and systems every day. Employees know what works and what doesn't. They struggle with tasks that should be simple. They recognize when the status quo just isn't working to meet current needs. They hear from customers when something is broken. But, often, those same employees keep doing what they have always done because they don't know how to make a change.

Fear of failure

One of the biggest barriers to innovation is the fear of failure. This can happen when employees see their co-workers disciplined or even let go because they try something new or make a decision that isn't aligned with the current best practice and the results aren't what was expected. It's important for businesses to support innovation by allowing room for failure while seeking opportunity for growth.

Reframing failure as a step towards improvement can lead to new ideas, fresh perspectives and ultimately new possibilities if it is managed well. To encourage innovation without fear, provide a safe forum for generating ideas such as facilitating brainstorming sessions, focus groups, discussion sessions and opportunities for input free of negativity and judgement.

Explore as a team the potential for success, but don't dismiss the learning opportunity for failure. Not every idea will work and even those that seem like a perfect fit might fall flat. Remember, the team that succeeds together also fails together. Learn from the failure. Discuss it. Build on it or go a different direction. If employees are comfortable with trying and failing and trying again, then they will seek innovation instead of finding a comfortable rut and keeping the business firmly stuck in it.

Providing room to innovate

If you don't know why you do something a specific way, other than that is the way it has always been done, it's time to re-examine the process. It might be perfectly fine, or it could use an update. It might not even be necessary at all. The best way to make changes is to create an environment that encourages innovation.

- **Provide multiple ways to share ideas.** An online form, in person discussions, an anonymous drop box, even email, are great ways to share improvement ideas.
- **Provide innovation time or activities to allow people to focus on being creative.** Remember that creativity doesn't necessarily happen on a schedule so flexibility is important.
- **Make it clear that innovation belongs to everyone.** It's easy for employees to think innovation belongs to people in creative careers such as marketing or product development, but innovative ideas come from the people working with processes and procedures every day and can identify the roadblocks and solutions to resolve them.
- **Test ideas in quick and simple ways before embarking on a big change.** Starting small is a good way to build towards a large change.
- **Include leadership in the innovation path.** When leaders are involved, employees know their ideas will be considered and acted on when possible.

- **Encourage ongoing communication around ideas.** Innovation doesn't happen at one time during a special week or day. It can come from random thoughts that occur as processes are taking place. Make sure the forum to communicate those ideas is always available.
- **Have clear expectations for idea generation.** This includes having a clear understanding of the problem being solved, how the suggestion solves the problem, and who the idea impacts. This will help lead to well-thought-out solutions that have the best chance of implementation.

Take action

The best way to kill innovation is to take a good idea and snuff it. Sometimes this happens due to workload or competing priorities, but innovation should always be a top priority.

Companies that are rigid and stagnant may not survive. Innovation is the future so act on ideas and let employees participate if possible. Create an innovation plan that is sustainable, measurable and supported. Then embrace the change and help employees do that same. The company's bottom-line will thank you.

Chapter 12:
Do the right thing

When ethics comes up in a conversation about business, the discussion often leads to hand wringing and head scratching. After all, ethics in business is an oxymoron, isn't it? Business is about being number one, beating the competitor, making the largest profits—no matter what.

We see it on TV every day. An advertisement on television for a business consulting firm praised the efforts of a young department manager who had impressed his superiors by increasing company profits. He did so by reducing the amount of product actually delivered to the customer by an unnoticeable amount.

If you think this sounds far-fetched, visit your local cereal aisle and take note of the shrinking box sizes. Note that the prices are not shrinking. Less product plus higher price equals greater profits. Good ethics? Not really. Good for the bottom line? Of course.

We see it in the actions of businesses. Take the average going-out-of-business sales. If you compare discounted prices at the failed store with those at competitors, the competitor prices will generally be lower. Liquidators tend to raise product prices when managing a going-of business sale to net the highest profits for creditors. As the store closure date comes closer, prices will drop to slightly below or the same as those of competitors. Is it ethical? If the store owes you money, it may seem so. If you are a consumer and you bought a high-priced item thinking you were getting a deal, you certainly feel cheated.

But are ethics and business truly incompatible? I say no. Not only are they compatible, but in today's competitive business environment, I feel ethics is necessary to build a healthy, customer-service oriented business.

What is ethics?

It's easy to hide behind, "It's just business." But businesses are built by people. And ethical decisions are ultimately personal decisions.

Ethics is judging right from wrong. Your judgment may be grounded in values instilled in you by family, church, community, and the laws and standards that govern society. These shouldn't be the sole basis of ethical decisions, since unethical practices exist even in the most righteous institutions.

You choose your day-to-day behavior and way of living based on the impact of these values in your life. In business, ethics materializes in the values your business brings to the marketplace. It's the way you treat your employees, customers, vendors, and community. Like children looking to their parents to guide them in their decision making, business owners look to their peers. But when those peers are acting contrary to the good of their constituents, ethical businesses need to step up and lead.

To determine if an action is ethical, ask yourself these questions:

- Does it serve the greater good of society?
- Is it fair?
- Is it honest?
- Is it a right that all people should have?

If you can answer yes to these questions, you can feel comfortable with your action. If you answer no to any of the questions, take a step back and analyze the action more completely before moving forward.

Ethics in action

A friend of mine went to the local farmers market and bought 12 ears of corn. When he got home and counted the corn he found he had fourteen ears of corn. He asked the farmer about this and the farmer said that he depended on return business. The extra ears of corn were seen by his customers as a reason to buy from the small farmer rather than the large grocery store.

This farmer took a customer service centered approach to business. He went the extra mile to treat his customers fairly and honestly. While he certainly benefited by the purchases of return customers, his goal was to provide his customers with extra value while encouraging them to purchase from the small farmers that served the marketplace. Does his action serve the greater good of society? Sure. His customers have extra corn for their dinner plates and other small farmers may see a financial return from the farmer's goodwill gesture.

On the flip side, Dave the painter suffered the results of bad ethical decision making. Dave worked for a paint company. He was asked to provide an estimate to a homeowner who wanted a fresh coat of paint on his house. When Dave arrived at the house, he was faced with a disgruntled resident who upon discovering what company Dave represented said he would never work with the paint company ever again. Why? His mother had hired another painter from the company who failed to complete the job as requested. The painter didn't scrape old paint or paint behind bushes. Dave offered to remedy the situation, but the customer gave a not-so-polite, "No, thank you."

The ethical lapse by painter number one trickled down to other members of the company. The original painter was dishonest when he didn't complete the work according to the customer's expectations. His one dishonest action tainted the reputation of the company as a whole. And angry customers vent. They talk to family and friends. They even post their frustrations on websites dedicated to highlighting bad business practices. As a result, bad business is bad for business.

Putting ethics into practice

Ethics can be tied to business goals. If the goal is to win market share at any cost, then cutting corners may be acceptable to that business. However, if the goal is to provide a good living for yourself and your employees through repeat and new customers, then treating people right appears to be part of the formula. Ethics in business could be summed up as treating other people the way you would want to be treated by them.

An ethical business makes its practices apparent to employees, customers and vendors. Businesses can do this through a mission statement, visions statement, and even an organizational credo. Internal policies and procedures outlined in the employee manual or other documentation also ensure that the company's way of doing business is obvious.

Industry guidelines also provide a reference for companies when making difficult ethical decisions. For example, Generally Accepted Accounting Practices (GAAP) are standards and rules for accounting professionals to follow to ensure they are providing above-board services. Medical professionals take an oath to do no harm. Realtors also follow a code of ethics established by their national association.

Ultimately, the responsibility for ethical behavior lies with the individual. Guidelines, rules and common practices help in the decision-making process, but only through personal action can one truly put ethics into practice.

An organizational credo

An organizational credo is a concise statement that reflects a company's core values, guiding principles, and ethical commitments. It serves as a moral compass for decision-making, employee behavior, and customer interactions. By clearly articulating what the organization stands for, a credo helps build trust, unity, and purpose across all levels of the business. Here is an example:

Our credo

Our organization values honesty in its leaders, employees, and partners. All transactions must be on the up-and-up. Information must be presented accurately, business arrangements must be made openly and in an environment of mutual understanding, and daily operations must be carried out with integrity.

Vendors will be held to the same level of honesty as the rest of the organization. Company employees will not do business with vendors who encourage questionable practices.

Employees also will not perform questionable practices if requested by our customers. Honesty leads to trust. Trust leads to an organization whose employees are proud to contribute towards the organization's success.

Our organization believes in openness through knowledge sharing. Knowledge sharing means learning from the past and sharing that information with others. It means placing information in the hands of all who need it, not just a few. The company will encourage questions and open discussion at all levels of the organization. The organization's leaders will provide open forums on a regular basis to share company information and field questions. Managers will share information with their employee groups. And employee groups will share information with each other.

Our organization believes in advocating for the customer. A transaction that ends with a satisfied customer is a successful transaction. The company will provide each employee with the training and authority they need to be attentive, knowledgeable and courteous. It will provide product reviews and customer information to keep employees up-to-date. Company leaders will train employees to manage difficult situations through one-on-one training and situational learning opportunities. They will also trust employees to make decisions in the best interest of the customer. Company employees will listen to customers, learn about their needs, and respond with respect, concern and kindness.

Example: Trade show trouble

Penny arrived at the Anaheim Convention Center with a suitcase of textbooks and a quota to meet. Her employer, a small Midwest textbook publisher, charged her with introducing the company's product, career-focused books, to the national education market and collecting a contact list of at least 50 prospective buyers.

Penny was a freelance editor for the company with some marketing responsibilities. Her background was education, having been a business teacher for several years before leaving teaching to start a family. She stayed connected to education through her freelance work and looked forward to the occasional sales trips for the publishing company.

Sales trips usually involved visiting schools to share the newest books in the series or delivering orders. Trade shows were a new experience. But Penny was excited. The prospect of raising the company's profile among educators, educational publishers, and distributors was a job she took on with pride.

She wheeled her suitcase into the great hall and found her booth position. It was near the back of the hall at the end of a row of small publishing companies similar in size to her own. The larger publishers and distributors had floor space at the center and front of the hall and the school representatives filled space at the sides of the room.

The convention was two-days of networking, gathering promotional materials, and getting to know the industry players. Penny had a sign-up sheet located at her booth to take prospects' names and numbers. On the first day of the convention all went well. Penny flipped through textbooks pages for interested visitors endlessly until her thumbs were numb. She educated teachers about the importance of preparing students for the careers of the future, and she courted distributors who could broaden the reach of the business.

At the end of the first day, she dropped onto her hotel bed, exhausted from the day's activities, but positive about the contacts she had made. She looked at her list of prospects. It numbered 35, a great result for the first day of the conference. She went to bed happy and looked forward to day two.

Day two was more of the same, but some of the acquaintances Penny made on day one returned for more specific information. She handed out order forms to many return visitors and collected additional contact information. As the day wound down, businesses started tearing down their booths and packing up to leave. Penny did the same.

Because Penny was new to the trade show circuit, she wasn't wise to the tricks employed by some industry competitors. She saw wandering presenters peering into booths but thought nothing of it. She tucked her promotional brochures, papers, and contact list into the front pocket of the suitcase. She then packed up her product samples and tucked her booth into its storage bins. After packing up the booth, she left the convention hall to call the airline and check on the status of her flight.

She was gone for about 15 minutes and when she returned, she noticed her suitcase was askew. Brochures were scattered on the floor and her contact list was missing—swiped by a malicious competitor. Penny's heart sank. She had gathered her quota of prospect contact information and it was now gone. Devastating thoughts raced through her head. She imagined her employer barring her from future trade shows, cutting her hours, or worse—firing her. Her mood, which had been bright just 15 minutes earlier, turned dark. As she stood circling around in the emptying convention center, she lost faith in the honesty of the human race.

She gathered up her luggage and left the trade show floor. She had one stop to make before catching a cab to the airport—the trade show office. She wasn't about to let a bad deed go unreported. Her list was lost, but she hoped that by reporting the incident she could encourage better protections or warnings for future trade show participants.

The office was buzzing with activity as the staff made arrangements to close out the show. Janitors came and went as the shift changed, floor managers listened to babble over their headsets, and administrative staff coordinated paperwork for teardown crews.

Penny stopped at the front desk. The clerk smile and asked, "Can I help you?"

"Yes," said Penny. "I had a contact list that I generated during the trade show and it was stolen from my booth."

"Oh, that's not good," said the clerk with a sympathetic smile. "Let me call the trade show manager for you." She summoned the manager to the front. The manager appeared promptly and shook Penny's hand.

"I hear you had a problem with your list."

"Yes," said Penny. "It was stolen from my bag. It had all my contacts from the show."

The trade show manager frowned. "This happens from time to time. We do what we can to stop it, but it always seems that there are one or two bad apples in the bunch."

The manager reached behind the entry desk. She pulled out a stapled packet of paper.

"Here," she said handing it to Penny. "This is the contact list for everyone who attended the trade show. This should make up for the contact information that was stolen. I really hate to see this kind of thing happen and wish there was more I could do to stop it. Your best bet going forward is to keep all your documents in a locked box that stays with you."

"I'll remember that," said Penny.

When Penny returned home after her trip, she left the list with her employer and trucked off to the office store to buy a lock box. She had learned her lesson the hard way that some businesses cheat their way to the top. Some may get caught, some may ultimately fail, and some may get away with it. But the risk isn't worth taking when a business's reputation, customer base, employee satisfaction, and financial strength are on the line.

Conclusion

Entrepreneurs form ideas, dream big, and make plans for the future. But we also must learn to mitigate risk. Even business schools teach techniques for assessing risks in the business environment. And businesses use these techniques to limit the potential for financial losses.

But risk is a part of entrepreneurship. Yes, you can plan your marketing strategy, your budget, and your business structure. But the future is uncertain. You may fail or you may succeed beyond your wildest dreams. Managing risk in business is necessary, but avoiding all risk is debilitating.

Imagine a parent who is so obsessive about safety they wrap their children in 24/7 safety nets—helmets to walk down the driveway, bars on beds, and shatterproof everything. Now imagine applying similar risk avoidance measures to a new business. The business would strangle itself with the helmet strap.

On the flip side is risk-taking at all costs. Thoughtless risk taking may lead to quick gains followed by huge losses. Decisions made on impulse can lead to oops moments. Some are recoverable, but those that break laws, violate customers' rights, or show disregard for shareholders, investors, or employees can spell doom for a fledgling business.

So, what's an entrepreneur to do? Practice an ounce of prevention or throw caution to the wind? Both and neither.

To be an entrepreneur you must dive into business challenges with gusto. Be bold. Be adventurous. It takes a vivacious spirit to put yourself out to the whims of the marketplace. Be a daredevil. But know what you are getting into and plan accordingly. Start by knowing your product and market, keeping organized records and managing your finances wisely.

Build trust in your business by developing ethical policies and procedures for working with employees and providing quality service to customers. Communicate clearly to keep your market informed. Hire the right people and remember to review your business plan on occasion to make sure you are heading in the right direction.

When you face losses take the risk to explore new opportunities, modify your marketing plan, and adjust failed processes. When you make big wins, cheer. But also review your practices on an ongoing basis to make sure they remain success drivers. And monitor customer relationships to head off potential threats.

And remember you're an entrepreneur. You are a risk taker by your very nature. You have drive, commitment, and spirit. You may fail, you may succeed, but at least you took the trip. And what an incredible trip it is.